Ancient Aliens to Modern UFOs:
The Disclosure Revolution

Adil Bhatti

Copyright © 2025 Adil Bhatti

All rights reserved.

No part of this book may be reproduced, stored in a retrieval system, or transmitted in any form or by any means—electronic, mechanical, photocopying, recording, or otherwise—without the prior written permission of the author, except in the case of brief quotations used in critical articles or reviews.

This book is a work of nonfiction reflecting the author's opinions, interpretations, and research. While historical documents, religious texts, and publicly available government materials are referenced, the author's conclusions represent personal viewpoints. Any resemblance to real individuals, events, or locations beyond those discussed factually is coincidental.

All images, quotes, and references remain the property of their respective owners and are used under Fair Use for commentary, criticism, or educational discussion.

First published 2025

TABLE OF CONTENTS

Chapter 1: "They" Don't want you talkin' about it. 1

Chapter 2: The Ones Who Visited 12

Chapter 3: Reading Scripture Differently 27

Chapter 4: They Never Stopped Coming 48

Chapter 5: Roswell and the Birth of Denial 82

Chapter 6: Modern Era Encounters 102

Chapter 7: Disclosure: The Moment is Here 135

Chapter 8: So... What Now? 156

About the author: 168

This book is dedicated to the brave men and women who refused to stay silent and shared their UFO/UAP evidence despite being mocked and insulted and ridiculed. Thank you for standing your ground and speaking the truth.

This book is also dedicated to my beautiful and wonderful children. I love you more than anything else!

"I am convinced that UFOs exist because I've seen one." - *Jimmy Carter: 39th President of the United States of America*

CHAPTER 1

"THEY" DON'T WANT YOU TALKIN' ABOUT IT

Why is this topic drowned under useless noise?

Can we stop scrolling just for a second, please? I mean seriously, put down your fancy smartphone or tablet... unless of course you're reading this book on your device. But in all seriousness, what I'm asking you to do is just to push the pause button on whatever it is you're doing right now. Something's been eating at me on the inside and I wanna share it with you.

While we all constantly waste valuable time following the tastiest celebrity gossip, the latest political drama, or whatever other manufactured crisis the news networks have decided to feed us this week, something truly massive has been taking place right under our noses... or maybe I should say, right over our heads. And I mean it is **MASSIVE**. It's the kind of thing that should be breaking news every single day on every single channel in every single country. The type of thing that should make you stop whatever the heck you're doing and take a closer look.

The United States government along with other governments of the world has quietly, almost casually, admitted that unidentified objects are regularly violating our airspace. These are not drones from some enemy nation. They're not weather balloons or experimental aircraft. This is not freakin' swamp gas. These are objects in the sky and also in the oceans that completely change our ways of understanding physics. These objects are operated by... well, we don't know what or who. Or maybe we do, and they're just not telling us. I'm sure it's the latter! They probably know to a certain extent.

Military pilots, people with years of training, people who fly around in multi-million dollar aircraft for decades, people whose job is literally to know what's up there in the sky, have gone on record describing things they can't explain, moving in ways which they also cannot explain. Declassified government documents exist. You can read them yourself. Congressional hearings have taken place where government and military officials have testified under oath about these encounters. Government has archives in the National Archives. Government even created something called "Project Blue Book" to study this aerial phenomenon. If they don't believe in UFOs, why would they officially be studying them? Something needs to be real for you to study it, right? At least you have to believe it's real.

And then... BOOM! Nothing! Your screen is drowned under the latest Netflix series or YouTube Shorts video and links upon links of useless crap to purchase online.

The stories surface for a day, maybe two. You might see a headline. You might click on it, maybe you don't. And then it vanishes, buried under the next celebrity scandal, the next political outrage, the next thing *they* want your mind focused on.

Back to normal and back to the online circus, guys! La-dee-da, everything is just fine and dandy!

Does that make any sense to any of you? Why the F is this not the ONLY thing we're talking about?

I'm gonna tell you why. But, be warned: you that you might find this all very bizarre and very disturbing.

Why They're Hiding It

First of all, I want you to know that I consider you my friend. You are reading my book and I truly appreciate that from the bottom of my heart. So... Hello, friend!

I'm going to give you three reasons, which, in my opinion, are the main reasons why this story keeps getting buried under all this useless social media crap. Each of the following reasons is terrifying in its own manner.

Reason One: The Technology Race

Okay, imagine this. You're the government... any government, it doesn't matter which one. American, French, Pakistani, Chinese... whichever! You suddenly get your hands on some extremely advanced technology... And when I say advanced, I don't mean just human advanced, I mean it's ADVANCED on another freakin' level. Imagine that it is advanced by several millennia, not just mere centuries. How do you tackle this problem? How do you handle alien technology when you have it in your possession?

What do you do? What's the next course of action?

Do you call a press conference and share it with the world? Do you hand it over to some scientists for open and public research? Or do you lock it in the most secure facility you have and throw every resource you've got at trying to figure out how it works so that you can use it to your own advantage? Wouldn't you want to make a profit from advanced technology, like we already do?

The thing is, whoever cracks this technology first doesn't just get an edge in the next conflict. No. They reshape this planet and its society entirely. Imagine having aircraft that can move at speeds we currently think are impossible. Imagine energy sources that make oil obsolete. Imagine propulsion systems that make space travel as simple as driving to your local Walmart in your Subaru.

Would you share that tech with others?

Wouldn't you want your government scientists to figure out how this technology works before any of our enemies do? Yes, obviously. You would keep it quiet and secretive until you knew how to use it to your advantage.

This isn't conspiracy theory stuff, people. This is basic geopolitics. This is how countries have always operated. They kept the Manhattan Project, developing the atomic bomb, a total secret from the American public and from also most of the government. What else could they be hiding?

Reason Two: They don't want you to know how powerless they really are

The uncomfortable truth is a hard pill to swallow. But still, please let this following part sink into your noggin.

These flying objects travel through our most restricted airspace frequently. They've been spotted over nuclear facilities multiple times.

They easily outmaneuver our most advanced fighter jets and essentially leave them behind in the dust. They have been described by pilots as accelerating at extreme speeds and then coming to a sudden stop. And then shooting off in the opposite direction also at mind-bending speeds. All of this would turn our regular human pilots into toothpaste because of the extreme G-force.

And the worst part about all of this is that the military cannot stop them from invading our airspace. They can do NOTHING about it.

Nothing!

Our country, the United States of America, has the most sophisticated radar systems, advanced aircraft and most powerful military, navy and air force on Earth. We Americans pay a lot of tax for the military to defend us. Yet whatever these things are in the sky, they come and go in our airspace as they please. We cannot catch them. We cannot intercept them. We cannot stop them. It begs the question: then why are we paying so much tax?

The government's main reason is to protect its people and keep them safe from external dangers. To be in control of what happens within their borders. So what happens when they have to stand in front of the public and admit, " *Yeah, so like, there's something in our skies, and like, we have absolutely no control over it*"?

The illusion of security and safety totally shatters. The emperor is caught with his pants down. Isn't that shameful and embarrassing?

They cannot allow that happen. Nope. No freakin' way! They can't admit that level of powerlessness. So they deflect, deny, downplay, and divert as best as possible. They change the subject and they keep us focused on threats they *can* handle, or at least have the *appearance* to handle, while this bigger, stranger reality plays out above our heads.

Reason Three: Everything Changes

This is the big one. This is the one that keeps me up at night, pondering and pondering more.

If this is real, and if we're not alone, if we've *never* been alone, if intelligent beings have been visiting Earth for thousands of years, then everything changes.

Everything.

Religion will have to adapt and rewrite itself due to major discrepancies and inconsistencies. Human history? Well, We have to reexamine it from the beginning. Our scientists will have to admit there have been many things we completely missed or completely misunderstood. Our entire understanding of what it means to be human, where we originate from, where we fit into the universe/multi-verse... all of it gets flipped upside down.

The uncomfortable part of all this is that all the people in power, all of these institutions we're supposed to trust, they all depend on us believing *their* version of reality. Your governments, your religious leaders, your corporations, your academic institutions. All of them maintain authority by being the ones with all of the answers. They're the experts, as they claim. They're the ones in control. That all changes with disclosure. People will lose faith in the world order and how it currently is. There will be huge changes everywhere.

Full disclosure doesn't just change what we know, it also changes who we trust. It changes what we believe in and it destabilizes the entire current social order. It pushes the reset button on our minds so that we can start over.

Some people would celebrate that while many others would panic. Many would demand accountability—" *You knew? You knew this whole time and you lied to us?*" All in all, there would be a lot of chaos and panic created. That is why you aren't supposed to hear about any of this.

Can you imagine the fallout? The absolute panic and chaos and anarchy? The complete restructuring of society?

So they keep us distracted... they give us endless drama to obsess over. They let the UFO story pop up just enough to satisfy the curious, and then bury it again under the next political crisis, the next Hollywood scandal, the next shiny brand-named item that they need us looking at.

But the Evidence Is There

Let's talk about what they can't hide: the evidence is there. It's always been there. It really just needs a good and hard look-see. It's time we dig even deeper.

Ancient cultures were not only separated by only huge distances, but also by thousands of years between them. There is evidence found in ancient texts from these cultures that describes basically the same thing. Visitors from the sky. It's in religious scriptures and texts that talk about beings descending from the heavens in vehicles of light and fire. It's found in military documents that have been declassified and available to view. It's in sworn testimonies from credible and trained observers who have nothing to gain and everything to lose by coming forward. This is not conspiracy theory, everyone. All it requires is a closer look.

Once I took a closer look and saw it, I could not then unsee it.

So that's what you and I will be doing, as friends, in this book. We're going to be taking a look at the evidence together as buddies and we will not treat this as some dry academic exercise. Let's talk about this, you and I. Together. Okay, friend?

Look At the World Differently With These 3 Questions:

Let's start our journey by asking three fundamental questions, which everyone should be asking, but almost nobody is.

Question One: Have they always been here?

We're going to be digging into ancient history. We're going to look at some civilizations that had no contact with each other due to being thousands of miles apart, but somehow described the exact same phenomena. We're going to read texts from thousands of years ago that sound less like mythology and more like eyewitness accounts of technology and alien contact. We're going to some important questions. What did our ancestors actually see? Were they describing something magical or technological?

Question Two: What are we seeing now?

We're going to also examine some modern-day encounters. We now have military footage that's been declassified and available for the public. We have pilot and Naval officer testimonies that are on the record.

We're going to be checking out several incidents that involve eyewitness accounts, radar confirmation, as well as physical evidence. We all want to know what's happening in our skies by asking very simple questions: what is this? WTF is this?

Question Three: Why has it been hidden?

We're going to trace the history of government involvement. This will include official denials, and the slow, grinding process of UFO disclosure that's happening right now. We want justified answers to several questions such as: why have they been hiding this? What exactly are they still hiding behind their closed doors? What will happen when the truth is revealed?

What I'm Asking of You

Look, my friend, I want you to be sure that I'm not here to tell you what to believe. *I'm really NOT.* You have the power to shut this book right now and throw it into the trash.

In this book, I would like to show you what they've been hiding. I will also show you some of the evidence and we will take a slow walk through some historical events after which you can draw your own conclusions. You can be the judge. You're obviously intelligent.. I mean you got this book, didn't you? (*wink.)

What I will ask is that you come into this with an *open mind...* not a gullible mind.

You should be questioning everything, including what I'm saying to you and think as critically as you can. But just try and keep an *open mind* so that we can continue looking for evidence together. We cannot stop asking questions and we cannot accept the official story and move on. Don't let that be you. Not for this topic or any other.

So what exactly is the official story? Well, it's been changing... quietly and slowly, but it's been changing. Our same government which spent billions of dollars and several decades creating lies about UFOs is now admitting that they actually exist. UFOs have been re-branded as UAPs, Unidentified Aerial Phenomena. Previously they were called flying saucers and even prior to that they were chariots to gods.

Ready?

Admittedly, all of this is extremely heavy stuff, and I don't mean to burden you with it. I hope to take a very chill approach with you, my dude, or my lady. I know its easier to avoid complicated discussions. I know all of that. But there are very important questions that are lingering and need answers. As you go down this path of questions, you will find even more questions. You will start connecting dots and wondering how come more people don't talk about this on a regular basis. It happened like that to me. So DO NOT read any further if you don't want this to happen to you.

And maybe you'll also start asking the three questions they don't want you to ask. Maybe.

The age of disclosure seems to be coming closer and closer. Will the COMPLETE TRUTH be disclosed during our lifetimes?

So here we go, ladies and gentlemen. Let's start at the very beginning. I want you to travel through time with me. We are going to go backwards many thousands of years to simpler times when our ancestors looked up at the heavens and saw something inexplicable. Something that really terrified them, yet inspired them. Something that changed them forever. Something which they decided to record on scripture and on walls because it was so absolutely extraordinary.

So, let us move forward. Let's talk about the visitors from above.

CHAPTER 2

THE ONES WHO VISITED

Alright, folks. Let's start our imagination engines. Please try hard to picture this.

Take yourself backwards in time between 4000 to 6000 years ago. That's a really, really, really long time ago. Now picture yourself standing either in the middle of a desert, or maybe a jungle clearing, or possibly a grassy plain. You can choose any of those settings, it doesn't matter. It goes without saying that there are absolutely no automobiles driving around on the ground, there are absolutely no airplanes in the sky, there is no heavy machinery or hum of electricity. None of that will exist for many thousands of years to come. The sounds you might hear could be your campfire crackling, or the slow whooshing of a river nearby, or simply the wind in your ear. The clothes you wear at this time are extremely simple. They may only cover your the groin area or private parts.

In the evening hours when the sun goes down, the darkness that you experience is *absolute*. It's not the kind of darkness that we are used to today, with all the street lights and the smartphone screens that illuminate our faces. I mean it is total and absolute darkness, baby! The kind where you can't see your hand in front of your face kinda darkness.

And then you look up.

The sky is everything. Our ancestors depended upon it. It is an important tool, almost like your mobile device is for you today. They used to track the moon's phases as calendar reference. They would use the sky as their clock, compass, and even the connection to the divine. In the clear and crisp night sky, you find billions of stars blazing across the heavens. You find the Milky Way stretching overhead like… well, a way of milk.

Now imagine something appears in that sky that doesn't belong there.

Something that moves wrong or something that shines too bright. Something that defies everything you understand about how the world works.

What would you do? How would you possibly explain it? How would you remember it?

You would find ways to share it with people. Like telling a story to the children and to others. You would find ways to record it like in a book or maybe on a wall of a temple for all others to see. You would want others to know that you saw something impossible and incredible and that it should not be forgotten.

And that's exactly what our ancestors did.

The started making records.

The Sumerians: Beginnings Of A Pattern

Our journey begins in ancient Mesopotamia, which we currently called Iraq. The year is approximately 4500 BCE. This is the region where one of humanity's greatest civilizations emerged: The Sumerians. But why should we take a deeper look at the Sumerians? Well, they didn't slowly develop over centuries in that region. They kind of just... appeared. Their origins are very mysterious. The Sumerian language has no known linguistic relative. Even historical linguistics cannot trace the origin of the Sumerian people through their language. Just to give you an example using a totally unrelated ethnic group, historical linguistics can track the origins of Kurdish people by studying how the Kurdish language evolved and by comparing it with both ancient and modern Iranian languages to reconstruct its descent from Proto-Iranian, which is the ancient ancestor of all Iranian languages. Aside from that mystery, the Sumerians created the first written language. They also created cities. There's advanced mathematics involved. There's astronomy that's so sophisticated it wouldn't be matched for thousands of years to come. The Sumerians had organized government, agriculture, architecture, and even art.

But where does all this originate? It suddenly showed up? How did that happen?

The Sumerians created the cuneiform system of writing, which is basically using a reed stylus and making wedge-shaped marks into soft clay. They wrote down all their important stuff like letters, legal documents, maps, literature and even religion in cuneiform script. We can still read those tablets today. Since they wrote down all their important stuff on clay, another thing they wrote about was visiting beings called the Anunnaki, which literally translates to "those who from heaven to Earth came." Think about it, the Sumerians found this topic important enough to put it on record. Also, the word "heaven" literally means "sky" in many cultures and languages.

So it's not "those who came from the mountains." It's not "those who came from across the sea."

From *heaven*... from the sky! At a time when there was no air travel or anything remotely close.

Ancient Sumerian texts mention how these beings brought valuable knowledge about irrigation techniques, about farming, building, and even how to organize society. They even shared secrets of mathematics and astronomy. They were described as powerful, technologically advanced, and not quite human. How interesting.

I'm not sure about you guys, but I think it's a little bit unfair to dismiss and neglect all this important information coming from the Sumerians about these visitors from outer space.

Another kicker in the story is that the Sumerians knew things that they should have not been able to know. They had detailed knowledge of our solar system. They knew about planets that wouldn't be "discovered" by modern science until we had telescopes much, much later on.

The Sumerians were able to track movements of planets with such incredible precision that it's just mind-boggling. They also understood concepts of mathematics which were way more advanced, even past the Bronze Age civilization that was much later in history. How?

Where did they receive this knowledge? Where did they get this info?

The Sumerians said it came from the sky from the Anunnaki. The visitors from the sky. The visitors who descended to Earth and told them.

You are welcome to believe that it's "just mythology" if you want. But it's mythology with some really specific, really accurate astronomical data attached to it. Kinda makes you wonder.

Ancient Egypt: The Precision That Shouldn't Exist

Now let's take a big jump thousands of miles over to Egypt. Use your imagination once again, please. You're living during 2500 BCE and the most advanced tool in your inventory is your good ol' trusty bronze chisel and hammer. The wheel is still relatively new technology. Basic arithmetic is your mathematical understanding.

Now... I request you to build me the Great Pyramid of Giza.

Go ahead. I'll wait.

If you are a construction worker in today's day and I take away all your tools and other instruments, can you construct that same pyramid with the same precision? I seriously doubt it. But somehow, *they did.*

The Great Pyramid isn't just big. That would be an insult to it. The thing is incredibly massive, made of about 2.3 million stone blocks, some weighing up to 80 tons a piece! I have actually visited the Great Pyramid and it is an engineering marvel which blows your mind when you lay your eyes on it. Even with a lot of slaves and ropes, to pull multiple mega-tons of rock upwards is beyond unbelievable.

It's already hard to believe that the pyramid was a staggering 480 feet, which is nearly 150 meters in height. Even more so is the precision with which it was built.

The base of the pyramid is level to within just 2.1 centimeters across a base that's 230 meters long. The sides are aligned to true north with an accuracy of 1/15th of a degree. The mathematical ratios encoded in its dimensions demonstrate knowledge of pi and the golden ratio. Are you trying to tell me they created the pyramid with that much accuracy and almost no mistakes made in its engineering... back in *those* days?

Try to put yourself in that time period again. Really rev up your imagination. There's no GPS. There are definitely no laser levels. Surely no computer calculations or artificial intelligence. No freakin' cranes or modern construction machinery whatsoever.

How? How did they manage that much accuracy and precision and manage all the weight without any kind of advanced tools or tech?

Besides all of this, the ancient Egyptians also left us with interesting texts and one of them is called the Tulli Papyrus. It describes an event that took place around 1480 BCE during the reign of Pharaoh Thutmose III that talks about "circles of fire" appearing in the sky. There were multiple objects which were bright, silent, and moving in formation. The text says that they were "more numerous than anything" and that even after several days, they ascended higher into the sky before disappearing. Should we just dismiss this as mythology too?

Another mystery to look at are the hieroglyphs at Abydos. Skeptics will say that these hieroglyphs. Are just overlapping from different time periods, and they could be right about that. But what I find weird is that there is a helicopter, a submarine and an airplane. When you really look at these in-person you have to wonder why these skeptics are so limited in their approach. I mean, the airplane's wings and tail are not like that of a bird... the Egyptians knew what birds looked like because they have hieroglyphs of them too... so it couldn't have been a bird... because it looks like an AIRPLANE!

Besides this, throughout Egyptian mythology, you have gods who descended from the sky. There was Ra traveling in his solar barque and other human-like beings coming down to interact with humans. They came down to teach them and to guide them. You find these during many eras of ancient Egypt and on walls of pyramids and other important structures, etc.

Does that sound familiar to you? Maybe like the Anunnaki from ancient Sumeria many thousands of years ago and from thousands of miles away? How curious.

South America: Messages for the Sky

Let's now swim across the ocean into the Americas. South America. Peru, to be exact. The Nazca Desert, even more exacter. Sometime between 500 BCE and 500 CE.

The Nazca people created something that makes absolutely no sense unless you consider visitors from the sky. They are called the "Nazca Lines" and they can only be seen if you are flying overhead. Check this out:

The Nazca Lines are what's known as geoglyphs, designs (BIG designs) carved into the desert ground. You will find several different designs. One's a hummingbird that's nearly 100 meters long. They have a massive spider and also a monkey, the one shown in the photo above. You can find a condor bird with a wingspan of over 130 meters. They are geometric shapes made to look like animals and other beings. They are lines that run perfectly straight for kilometers. By the way, there are over 700 of these giant carvings out in the desert.

As if all of that is not weird enough, the weirdest part is that if you're standing on the ground looking at these lines, they're just... well, lines. They look only like long grooves in the dirt. You cannot see the patterns, you just see straight lines because they are that long. You can't see the shapes of any creature. You have no idea what you're looking at except for a straight boring line.

You can only see them from the air.

If you are hundreds of feet up in the sky, suddenly these random lines become intricate, massive artworks. The hummingbird takes shape... the spider appears... all the patterns emerge.

But the Nazca people had no aircraft. There would be no airplanes or helicopters for another couple thousand years.

So who were they making these for? Who was supposed to see them? Some people say that they might have been made for irrigation purposes. But that doesn't make much sense, because why would they create giant shapes of creatures in the middle of the desert. If they were for irrigation, then it would probably just be in straight lines or grid formation but not in animal shapes. These are made for aerial viewing and appreciation from above. Were they trying to attract other flying beings to come down to the Peruvian desert by any chance? Sounds more reasonable than irrigation to me!

The mystery does not end with the Nazca Lines. Flip over to Cusco, to the fortress of Sacsayhuamán and you will find massive stones. Some of those stones weigh over 200 tons, yes, OVER 200 TONS each!! These monoliths were cut and fitted together with such precision that you can't slide a piece of paper between them. There was no use of mortar. It was just stone on stone, fitted so perfectly that the structures have survived massive earthquakes that destroyed everything else around them. How did they lift these megalithic stones? I don't care what you tell me about having slaves and ropes, but it is just unbelievable because rope cannot lift that much capacity and neither can a lot of men, along with keeping the exact accuracy of laser-cut precision into account as well. Please see AI ChatGPT response when I type in "how many men need to lift 200 tons":

Lifting 200 tons (approximately 181,437 kg or 440,924 lbs) is <u>far beyond human capacity</u>, requiring thousands of average men or <u>specialized machinery</u>.

If we then take a visit Puma Punku in Bolivia, you'll find stones with cuts so precise, so geometric, so *perfect* that they look like they're machine-made. There are right angles that are exactly 90 degrees, and I mean exact. They have surfaces that are flat to within millimeters across meters of stone. There are intricate and interlocking shapes that fit together like Lego blocks, which by the way are created using help of computers. These ancient people were cutting through rock with the accuracy of computers?

Remember, everyone: bronze chisels and stone hammers. Supposedly, that's all they had to work with. Yup.

Does any of this make sense to you? Should we continue our pattern of dismissing what's in front of our eyes?

There were other civilizations in different parts of the Americas. They were the Inca, the Maya, the Aztec. All of whom had stories about gods visiting from the sky. One god was Quetzalcoatl, who was said to come down from the heavens and teach humanity. Another god was Viracocha who brought down knowledge of agriculture and civilization. Yet another god was Kukulkan who promised he would return to Earth from the stars. All these various civilizations accredited their advancement to beings from the sky.

All just a coincidence? So much coincidence in different continents?

Indigenous Peoples: The Star People

This pattern isn't limited to the "famous" ancient civilizations.

There are Native American who have stories about "Star People" visiting them from the sky. The Hopi tribe have mentioned "The Ant People" sheltering them from cataclysms and teaching the humans how to survive. Even the Lakota tribe tell tales about how visitors from the stars came down to Earth to bring them wisdom and guidance.

We find evidence in Australia with Aboriginal rock art depicting figures known as the Wandjina, who similarly, came down from the sky.

One of the most incredible indigenous people are the Dogon tribe from Mali in Central Africa. This tribe had an unusual and very detailed knowledge of the Sirius star system, which includes the existence of a white dwarf star that cannot be seen with the naked eye, called Sirius-B. The Dogon tribe somehow were able to describe the star's orbital period as well as its density and, shockingly, its relationship to another star, Sirius-A! This African tribe, without the use of any telescopic equipment, was somehow able to confirm the existence of Sirius-B, even though science would not confirm its existence until 1862 and not photograph it until 1970. Another coincidence, eh?

But seriously, how did the Dogon know? Well, they said beings from Sirius visited them and taught them. Beings visiting from the heavens/sky.

The pattern repeats across continents. It also repeats across cultures which had no contact with one another due to obvious enormous distances and transportation constraints as well as the lack of communication equipment.

So the pattern is that beings from the sky visit, knowledge suddenly advances, technologies that seem impossible for the time appear. And always, *always*, the same message: we were taught by them. We were visited by beings from above and they showed us the way. They came from the sky.

The Teacher Theory

All of these things point to many questions.

What if these weren't just random visits? What if they were lessons? What if beings are coming down from wherever and are teaching us the good ways, the honorable ways, the ways of advancing, the peaceful ways.

Think about it. In ancient times, these visitors, whoever or whatever they were, showed up and taught our ancestors fundamental things. How to farm, how to understand the stars how to organize society, how to build structures that would last many millennia. They gave humanity the tools to survive and to advance.

In the next chapter we will move on towards Biblical times. It would be many thousands of years after all these ancient times of this current chapter. We will learn how people started calling these visitors "angels" from the heavens. Funny enough, these visitors were also guiding humans how to do good and how to treat each other well, how to have good moral codes and to have spiritual guidance. Doesn't that sound familiar to you?

But think about that word: "heavens." What did ancient people mean by that? They meant the sky. The place where the stars and sun and moon lived. If beings came from the sky, of course you'd say they came from the heavens. It's the same thing. I just want to you to be very clear in your understanding about this.

And if these beings had technology you couldn't understand, if they could fly, if they could do things that seemed impossible... wouldn't you think they were divine? Wouldn't you call them angels or gods? Ancient people looked at science as if it were magic or divine because they couldn't define or explain the technology at that time in the past. Maybe magic is simply misunderstood technology.

Now, please jump to modern times. We've got multiple documented accounts, and we're going to explore these in detail later in the book, of UFOs hovering over nuclear weapons facilities. In 1967, at Malmstrom Air Force Base in Montana, ten nuclear missiles went off-line while a glowing red object hovered over the facility. Similar incidents have been reported at other nuclear sites around the world.

What if it's the same thing? What if they're *still* teaching us the same thing?

In Ancient times: "Let me show you how to farm, how to construct, and how to survive."

In Biblical times: "Here's how to live peacefully and how to treat each other well."

In Modern times: "Stop. You're about to destroy yourselves. These weapons are too dangerous. Be more peaceful. Don't use bombs."

Doesn't the message sound so familiar across thousands of years of human development? Perhaps the message is coming from the same source. Guidance toward peace, knowledge, and our survival and perhaps our planet's survival?

Are they teachers? Are they guardians?

Do you feel like I'm connecting dots that shouldn't be connected?

I dunno, I really don't. But the pattern is there. It's hard to unsee it after you see it, that's for damn sure.

It's Hard to Ignore the Pattern

Look, I know what you're thinking. Come on, Mr B, none of this is concrete evidence, my dude! This ain't no smoking gun! The fact of the matter is that I have no alien spacecraft to show you. What I can show you is a pattern. I can show you things which are seemingly impossible, but have happened.

Various civilizations from all across the Earth were telling the same story. These civilizations were completely separated by time and distance and no simply no way to communicate between each other. Yet we find the same story from them all: beings from the sky brought knowledge and wisdom.

Structures being built with such extreme precision that it challenges our understanding of what was possible with ancient technology.

Astronomical knowledge that shouldn't exist yet.

Artwork that can only be appreciated from the air, well before human flight ever existed.

And always, running through it all like a thread, this idea of teachers from above. Guides. Visitors who showed humanity how to advance, how to survive, how to reach for something better.

You can dismiss it all as coincidence or as mythology. You can dismiss it as primitive people misunderstanding natural phenomena or exaggerating stories across generations.

Can all of it just be nothing more than mythology?

Are you trying to say that the Great Pyramid or the Nazca Lines or the Sumerian tablets which describe planetary orbits make perfect sense and there's no mystery involved?

I, unfortunately, cannot. And I don't think you can either. Nobody can as far as I can tell. What I can see are these patterns and they give me a reason to write this book. Oh, and by the way, I'm much obliged that you've been on this journey with me so far... High five!

What Comes Next

These stories of visitations didn't stay buried in ancient history, nor did they didn't fade away with forgotten civilizations.

They made it into humanity's most sacred texts. The Bible, The Holy Quran, and The Bhagavad Gita. These are some of the holiest religious scriptures that billions of people follow today.

If you really start to analyze these books, they will start sounding less like poetry and a lot more like eyewitness accounts of encounters with beings from above.

Things start to sound like technology.

So let's talk about what happens when sky visitors meet organized religion. Let's talk about angels, prophets, and vehicles descending from the heavens.

CHAPTER 3

READING SCRIPTURE DIFFERENTLY

Alright, you Beautiful people. As we step into the third chapter, I really need you guys to understand something.

Firstly, I want you to know that I'm a firm believer in God. I love God and I fear God. I respect you and I respect whichever religion you follow, whichever God(s) you worship. I'm not here to make a mockery of anyone's religion or their sacred texts. That's not what this is about... not even close.

All I'm trying to do is generate an idea. Please come into this chapter with an *open* mind. This is just an exploration. It is a "*what if???*" I don't claim to have religion figured out any more than the next person. In my personal opinion, I don't believe that any human has fully grasped the concept of God. The reason I say this is because if we hardly understand the planets in our solar system, let alone nebulas in outer space or even something as micro as the quantum world... how do we possibly expect anyone to believe that we understand God, the one who created all of it? I mean, wouldn't we have to first understand how every single thing around us, from the tiniest to the largest, works in order to understand its Creator? We have close to zero understanding of any of these things, and yet many of us, scholars included, claim to have understood God or the meaning of scriptures? Scriptures are meant to be the word of God. Nobody can possibly have understood them if we barely understand the universe around us, let alone about Him who created the universe around us. We try to grasp infinity with such finite minds. So please, keep an *open mind* in this chapter and very kindly do not take offense at my words. They are not meant to be harmful whatsoever. I appreciate you... thank you!

Let's get into it, shall we?

Could it be possible that the sacred scripts, which mention angels, divine messengers, and creatures of light... that all of these... beings... were not just spiritual metaphors. Could it be that these entities originating from beyond our realm had interactions with humans and those people portrayed them using the only language available at that time?

I'm not claiming this is absolutely accurate or that I fully understand what occurred. What I'm suggesting is: what if? Let's just entertain the "what if" for now and take it from there.

The Language Problem

Let's rev the engines of our imagination once again. Please visualize yourself 3000 years in the past. The highest level of technology available to you is perhaps a homemade knife or maybe a spear, possibly a simple digging tool. Whatever it is, it's something incredibly mediocre. You can totally forget about words such as "aircraft" or "spacecraft" or "extraterrestrial" because all of them are far beyond your understanding. Those concepts don't exist yet. You don't have a framework for understanding machines or advanced civilizations from other planets. The language of your time is steeped in the spiritual and the divine. If you see something in the sky, you would automatically consider it to be divine.

What else would you call the beings you encounter but angels or gods? That is the only language you know!

The sky/heaven was the place where God lived. So anything that came from the sky, by definition, came from the realm of the divine. Do you get it?

But what if these encounters were exactly what they appeared to be, alien and UFO visitations, and we've been interpreting them through a spiritual lens when maybe, just maybe, they were also physical events? If we have proof that UFOs are in our skies today, who's to say they have not been here thousands of years ago. Maybe they have ALWAYS been here! Maybe they were here long before humans.

We're going to start from the Holy Bible. A very magnificent text.

Ezekiel's Vision: A Close Encounter? Maybe?

I'm going to share a passage from the Bible with you, which I'd like you to read. And I mean REALLY read. My request to you is not to read it metaphorically. Take it as an event. An event so incredible that the viewer had to record it for others!

So let's open up our Bible. Oh, by the way, in case you don't have a Bible handy, don't worry, I do have the chapter down below. You can find it in the first chapter from the book of Ezekiel. Living in exile, Ezekiel was a prophet in Babylon around the year 593 BCE. One day he was by the Kebar River and he saw something that was just bewildering. I'm going to set the scene first and then share the complete text out of the Bible. You can be the judge of it yourself.

Imagine yourself as Ezekiel many thousands of years ago. It's just a regular ol' day from 3000 years ago consisting of simple tasks like farming or herding cattle. And then, suddenly, you see something in the sky. It seems like a storm brewing, but not any regular storm. This thing is massive! It's roaring towards you from the north. There's an enormous cloud, but it's glowing from within. Lightning is flashing everywhere. In the center of the storm is an intense glowing disc-shaped object.

You would think that this is crazy enough for poor old Ezekiel... but no! Things are about to get much worse!

Out of this storm, these... creatures emerge. Four of them. They look somewhat human, but they're not human. They are humanoid creatures that have four faces. One face is a human's face, the second is a lion's face, the 3rd is an ox's face, and the 4th is an eagle's face. They each have 4 wings with human-like hands underneath the wings. They have bright and shiny feet as well. But hold on to your horses, ladies and gentlemen. This isn't the weirdest part yet.

Next to each creature is, what looks like a wheel/disc. But

not a regular wheel, a wheel within a wheel, and the rims of these wheels are covered in eyes. Yes, eyes which are all around the rims. These wheels move with the creatures, moving up when the creatures move up and moving down when they move down. Watch out, Ezekiel!

Above these creatures is something that resembles a crystal platform, which is glowing. There is a throne on this platform with a man-like being sitting on the throne glowing like fire and surrounded by bright light.

Ezekiel is so horrified by what he sees that he collapses on the ground face down begging for mercy.

Wow, wasn't that intense? Let me share with you, word for word straight out of the Bible. I request you kindly to read it as if it's something that someone is describing in front of him. Please read it like a report. Here it is:

Ezekiel 1: Ezekiel's Inaugural Vision

1. *In my thirtieth year, in the fourth month on the fifth day, while I was among the exiles by the Kebar River, the heavens were opened and I saw visions of God.*

2. *On the fifth of the month—it was the fifth year of the exile of King Jehoiachin—*

3. *the word of the LORD came to Ezekiel the priest, the son of Buzi, by the Kebar River in the land of the Babylonians. There the hand of the LORD was on him.*

4. *I looked, and I saw a windstorm coming out of the north— an immense cloud with flashing lightning and surrounded by brilliant light. The center of the fire looked like glowing metal,*

5. and in the fire was what looked like four living creatures. In appearance their form was human,

6. but each of them had four faces and four wings.

7. Their legs were straight; their feet were like those of a calf and gleamed like burnished bronze.

8. Under their wings on their four sides they had human hands. All four of them had faces and wings,

9. and the wings of one touched the wings of another. Each one went straight ahead; they did not turn as they moved.

10. Their faces looked like this: Each of the four had the face of a human being, and on the right side each had the face of a lion, and on the left the face of an ox; each also had the face of an eagle.

11. Such were their faces. They each had two wings spreading out upward, each wing touching that of the creature on either side; and each had two other wings covering its body.

12. Each one went straight ahead. Wherever the spirit would go, they would go, without turning as they went.

13. The appearance of the living creatures was like burning coals of fire or like torches. Fire moved back and forth among the creatures; it was bright, and lightning flashed out of it.

14. The creatures sped back and forth like flashes of lightning.

15. As I looked at the living creatures, I saw a wheel on the ground beside each creature with its four faces.

16. This was the appearance and structure of the wheels: They

sparkled like topaz, and all four looked alike. Each appeared to be made like a wheel intersecting a wheel.

17. As they moved, they would go in any one of the four directions the creatures faced; the wheels did not change direction as the creatures went.

18. Their rims were high and awesome, and all four rims were full of eyes all around.

19. When the living creatures moved, the wheels beside them moved; and when the living creatures rose from the ground, the wheels also rose.

20. 20 Wherever the spirit would go, they would go, and the wheels would rise along with them, because the spirit of the living creatures was in the wheels.

21. When the creatures moved, they also moved; when the creatures stood still, they also stood still; and when the creatures rose from the ground, the wheels rose along with them, because the spirit of the living creatures was in the wheels.

22. Spread out above the heads of the living creatures was what looked something like a vault, sparkling like crystal, and awesome.

23. Under the vault their wings were stretched out one toward the other, and each had two wings covering its body.

24. When the creatures moved, I heard the sound of their wings, like the roar of rushing waters, like the voice of the Almighty, like the tumult of an army. When they stood still, they lowered their wings.

25. Then there came a voice from above the vault over their

heads as they stood with lowered wings.

26. *Above the vault over their heads was what looked like a throne of lapis lazuli, and high above on the throne was a figure like that of a man.*

27. *I saw that from what appeared to be his waist up he looked like glowing metal, as if full of fire, and that from there down he looked like fire; and brilliant light surrounded him.*

28. *Like the appearance of a rainbow in the clouds on a rainy day, so was the radiance around him. This was the appearance of the likeness of the glory of the LORD. When I saw it, I fell facedown, and I heard the voice of one speaking.*

Okay. Let's breath and stop for a second here.

Do me a favor and answer me this question. Wouldn't you somehow record this incident and share it with others if it happened to you?

An object approaches you from the sky. It's surrounded by clouds and lightning. There's intense light and what looks like glowing metal. There are beings inside, or associated with it, that move in coordinated fashion. There are mechanical-looking wheels covered in what Ezekiel describes as "eyes" (could those be lights? Windows? Sensors of some sort?). These wheels or discs move in perfect synchronization with the beings. There's a crystalline platform structure of some sort above them, and a throne-like seat that has a glowing humanoid figure sitting on it.

The sound? Like rushing water... like an army. It is overwhelming and loud.

No wonder Ezekiel collapsed to the ground out of fear. I would be trembling in my socks if it happened and probably crying like a baby.

Now, I'm not telling you this wasn't a divine vision. I'm not saying it wasn't God revealing himself to Ezekiel. But what if it was both? What if God works through creation like through beings, through technology that we can't comprehend and what if Ezekiel witnessed something real and physical that was also spiritually significant? What if it's both. What if God sends his message through other intelligent beings to us meager and moronic humans? I mean, we humans consider ourselves smarter than dogs. We try to teach dogs to be good and to be disciplined, etc. Wouldn't a smarter being always teach one who is less intelligent-er?

What if these "angels" slash aliens were piloting something? Maybe they do work for a higher power which has created us and they have certain duties to perform, like monitoring humans?

What if Ezekiel did see an actual spacecraft approaching? What if he described it the only way he could using the only language and concepts available to a person who was living 2600 years ago.

"Wheels within wheels." "Eyes all around." "Glowing metal." "Wings that sound like rushing water."

Does that sound like poetry or unexplained technology?

The Jinn: Islam's Concealed Beings

Now let's shift over to another sacred text. This time it's the Holy Quran. A beautiful and most wonderful text.

In Islamic tradition, there are beings called the Jinn. And

here's what's fascinating about them, the Quran is very clear that the Jinn are not metaphorical. They're not symbols or allegories.

What the Quran has to say about Jinn is that they are living beings and real creations of God. They make their own decisions, just like humans. The humans are made from clay, essentially from the Earth. Jinn were created from smokeless fire and have existed since before the humans. Some of the Jinn are good, while others are bad. They use their own free will to disobey or obey God's commands. God punishes them and rewards them accordingly, the same way he does to humans.

Besides all these incredible points in the Quran, the one I find most striking is that the Jinn can see humans, but the humans cannot see Jinn.

They're hidden. They are concealed. They are operating in a realm we cannot perceive.

Does this sound familiar to you? Maybe how aliens from today are hard to spot?

There's an entire chapter of the Holy Quran called Surah Al-Jinn (Surah 72). That literally translates to "Chapter of the Jinn". An entire chapter about intelligent life that's not human. Why would God do that unless He wanted us to know that we're not alone? That His creation is vast and varied and includes beings we can't fully see or understand? It is entirely dedicated to these beings.

Take a look at how eerily similar the Jinn sound to modern descriptions of extraterrestrial beings.

The Quran and Islamic tradition describe the Jinn as:

- A separate creation from humans, with their own

independent existence. They're not humans or angels. They're something else entirely. They are LIVING beings.

- **Created from fire or energy, not physical matter like humans.** The Quran says they're made from "smokeless fire." What if that's describing their appearance as not quite solid? What if "fire" is the closest word from the 7th-century for describing energy or plasma or something beyond earthly elements? What if we humans are made of clay (Earth) while they are made of smokeless flames... perhaps its describing elements of their planet the way clay is to Earth?
- **Able to see us, but we cannot see them.** They exist in a realm that's hidden from human perception. We share the same space, but they're concealed. How many UFO and alien encounter reports describe beings that seem to appear and disappear, that evade our detection systems, that operate just beyond our ability to fully perceive or capture them? How many times have people said, "It was there, and then it just... vanished"? How come we never really have hard concrete proof of aliens... maybe because it cannot be left behind? Is that some kind of technology that they have or something else entirely?
- **Limited capacity to fly through the sky.** The Quran describes the Jinn trying to eavesdropping on heavenly conversations, but they get driven away by "meteorites" or "shooting stars" when they fly too close. What if this is describing beings who can travel through space but are limited by cosmic barriers or cosmic laws? Do they maybe "watch" or "monitor" beings from different planets?
- **Jinn are not omniscient, despite having knowledge and abilities beyond those of humans.** They're advanced,

surely, but they're not gods of any sort. They cannot tell the future and they don't have access to divine secrets. They're powerful, yes, but limited.
- **Jinn are responsible for their own choices and decisions.** They have free will. Some follow God's guidance; others rebel. Sound like any other intelligent species you know? (Hint: humans.)

There is also mention in the Holy Quran about the time before Islam when polytheistic Arabs would worship the Jinn. These Arabs were fearful of them and revered them because the Jinn could do things that humans could not do. They had powers which seemed divine at the time. But the Quran does correct this misunderstanding and informs us that Jinn are NOT gods. They are living beings like humans, but not like humans. They are creations of God, but they come from a different realm.

Is it possible that the Jinn are what we call extraterrestrials today? Do you think God was informing us that "we are not alone" almost 1400 years ago? Perhaps God was letting us know that there are other intelligent beings in this universe. That some of these beings are really good peeps while others are just jerks.

And what if the reason we can't see them, the reason they're so good at hiding, the reason we have stories and encounters but no definitive proof, is because, as the Quran mentions, they exist in a way that's concealed from our normal perception? There is some sort of barrier which is undetectable by us humans. Is it some tech or are they on another inter-dimensional plane?

I mean come on! The Quran dedicates an entire chapter to these beings. It describes them in good detail. It acknowledges their existence as fact, not fiction. And it describes characteristics that sound remarkably similar to what modern UFO researchers and experiencers describe: advanced beings, hidden from most people's view, capable of incredible things, neither fully physical nor fully spiritual, operating under laws we don't fully understand. That really sounds eerily similar to ETs.

I'm not saying the Jinn are LEGIT aliens. I'm saying that it could be possible that the Quran was telling us about extraterrestrial life from the very beginning. Is it possible that our failure to see the Jinn is a good explanation why UFO and alien encounters are so elusive and so hard to capture? They might well be masters of concealment, just as the Quran describes.

The only thing I'm asking you to do is keep an *open mind*.

Vimanas: Flying Machines of Ancient India

Well, that's the Bible and the Quran out of the way. Let's travel through time before both of these books were written. We are going to ancient India. We will take a look at the Mahabharata and the Ramayana. These are epic poems and religious texts that date back thousands of years.

These texts describe something called Vimanas.

Vimanas are flying machines. They are not metaphorical chariots of the gods. They are not poetic descriptions of clouds or divine visions. They are actual flying vehicles, described in technical detail.

Is it just me who finds it unusual (and slightly disturbing) that there are texts thousands of years old, written well before the Wright Brothers and also long before Da Vinci sketched his flying machines, much earlier than humans had concepts of aerodynamics or aviation… that these texts from ancient India describe aircraft and possibly spacecraft in immense detail?

The texts are not vague either. Oh, no! They describe how these Vimanas worked.

Here's what the texts say about Vimanas:

Propulsion System: The texts describe these Vimanas as powered by a "mercury engine." Some accounts talk about gyroscopes, others mention electricity or solar energy. There are descriptions of propulsion systems that use a "whirlwind motion" set in motion by the power of heated mercury. Now, modern science knows that mercury has unique properties, it's liquid at room temperature, it's a conductor, it reacts to magnetic fields. Could ancient people have stumbled onto something? Or were they describing technology they had seen but didn't fully understand?

Capabilities: The descriptions of what Vimanas could do sound like something out of a science fiction novel, or out of a modern UFO report. These craft could ascend vertically. They could descend rapidly. They could travel at incredible speeds. They could change direction instantly, without turning. There are other texts describing Vimanas producing a "focused beam of light" which could be used as either a weapon or as a tool.

Does any of this sound familiar to you? To me, it sounds exactly like the way military pilots today describe UAPs, objects that perform impossible maneuvers, objects which accelerate instantaneously, seemingly able to defy both inertia and gravity. Seriously? Ancient texts from ancient India were talking about all of the stuff reported today? Hmmm... (*shrugs*) I'm sure it's probably nothing... right?

Control with mind: Some of these ancient texts also suggest Vimanas could be controlled *mentally* through the power of the pilot's mind. This is harder to dismiss as fantasy because we're currently developing brain-computer interfaces. Elon Musk's company Neuralink is working on tech that allows people control their devices with their thoughts. What if this isn't fantasy? What if it's a description of technology that ancient people witnessed. What if this is simply technology so advanced that it seemed like magic to the people from that time period?

Appearance: The texts describe Vimanas in various shapes. Some are tubular or cigar-shaped. Others are disc-shaped. Some have tail fins; others don't. Multiple shapes, multiple designs, almost exactly like the variety of UFO shapes that have been reported for decades across the world.

Let me tell you something else… there's a text called the Vaimanika Shastra, sometimes called the "Science of Aeronautics," which some interpret as an actual technical manual. It contains verses that describe the construction and operation of these flying machines. It talks about materials, about the energy sources, about their piloting techniques. WTF?

Skeptics will tell you this is all mythology, that it's religious symbolism, that ancient people were just imaginative storytellers. Sure. I'm sure they were that too, probably.

But then why are the descriptions so specific? Why do they include technical details? Why do multiple texts, separated by centuries, describe the same types of craft with the same capabilities? How come we have similar things to talk about now in this day and age?

And why do these ancient descriptions match so closely with modern UFO sightings?

I'm not saying ancient India had a space program. I'm not

saying humans built these Vimanas either.

But what if humans saw them? What if these craft visited ancient India, and the people there did exactly what Ezekiel did, exactly what people have always done when confronted with the inexplicable, they wrote it down. They tried describing what they saw using the words of at that time.

And what if those accounts are sitting in our sacred texts, waiting for us to read them with fresh eyes? Why can't we just open our minds a little bit more?

The Jewish Tradition: Meroz and the Stars

Moving onwards, friends! Isn't all of this exciting? Let's look at an example from Jewish tradition.

There is a brief but fascinating passage from the "Book of Judges" about a place that is called Meroz. A curse is pronounced on Meroz for failing to help in the fight after a battle has taken place. This is from the script:

"'Cursed is Meroz,' said the messenger of the Lord, 'cursed are its inhabitants,' because they came not to the aid of the Lord, to the aid of the Lord against the mighty." — Judges 5:23

Doesn't it sound like Meroz was a city that just didn't want to help? Yes, I think it does. But it gets interesting, don't worry. Let me tell you more.

The Talmud is the central text of Rabbinic Judaism and it offers an interpretation that Meroz might not be a place on Earth at all. One opinion, although disputed, in the Talmud (Mo'ed Katan 16a) identifies Meroz as a *star or a planet*.

It is defined as a celestial body, in space, and not as a human city. It is a planet or a star of some sort.

If we understand this correctly, Meroz is a star or planet, and it's being were cursed for not taking action. Doesn't that imply that there are *inhabitants* of that celestial body who have free will and can make choices and may be held accountable for their actions.

There have been a lot of Jewish sages who have grappled with this passage. Some, like Rabbi Pinchas Eliyahu Horowitz in his work Sefer HaBrit, have said that this is proof of existence of extraterrestrial life and intelligent beings on other worlds. Those beings, like humans, have the capacity to choose between right and wrong. Can you see any familiarity in this? (Hint: Jinn from the Quran.)

Let's think about that. Ancient Jewish scholars, hundreds of years ago, looking at this text and concluding: "This is talking about life on other worlds. That's what this is about."

It was not seen as science fiction. It was not portrayed as fantasy. It was based on theology and a legitimate interpretation of sacred text.

What if they were right? What if that is exactly what Meroz is? Why should it be so difficult to believe? We all know about how many countless bajillions of galaxies, stars, planets there are in the universe. Why, for the sake of God, could there not be a possibility that intelligent life came into contact with humans at some point and we recorded those incidents? Open minds, people! Open minds!

Buddhism: Infinite Worlds and Countless Beings

Before we connect all these dots, there's one more major world religion we need to talk about which is Buddhism. Buddhism has surprising things to say.

Buddhist cosmology describes something that sounds

remarkably like what we would call a multi-verse filled with extraterrestrial life.

Are you amazed yet?

Innumerable World Systems

In the Anguttara Nikaya, the Buddha describes the universe as containing "thousands of suns, thousands of moons, thousands of inhabited worlds of varying sorts and sizes."

Read that again. *Thousands of inhabited worlds.*

There is not just our one world, but thousands of worlds scattered across the universe, each has its own beings with their own way of life.

The Majjhima Nikaya (MN 3.123, the Acchariya-abbhuta Sutta) goes even further by describing an immeasurable light shining across various world systems when a Bodhisatta (enlightened being) descends into one of these many worlds.

Think about that carefully now. A light that appears across multiple world systems. Multiple worlds are aware of an event happening on another world. Communication or connection between these different inhabited places across the cosmos through light. Are they talking about laser communication? I dunno. You tell me.

This isn't modern sci-fi because it was written over 2500 years ago.

Realms Beyond the Human

Buddhist cosmology maps out numerous realms of existence beyond just the human realm. There are devas or heavenly beings, sometimes translated as "gods" but more accurately understood as advanced beings who exist in higher realms. There are asuras, sometimes called "anti-gods" or "titans." There are other beings in countless other states of existence.

According to Buddhist teachings, these are not just metaphors. They are real sentient beings. They go through life experiencing suffering, illness, and even death. They are not gods, but rather they exist on different realms. Buddhism has always assumed that we're not alone.

What Does This Mean?

Buddhism does not describe UFOs or ET visitors the way Ezekiel or the way Hindu texts might describe their Vimanas. Buddhism assumes, as a foundational principle, that the universe is vast beyond comprehension and it is completely filled with countless forms and varieties of life. It also teaches us that whatever world its inhabits live on, they're subject to the same universal truths and the same laws. The same fundamental nature of reality.

Connecting the Dots

Okay! Phew! That was heavy!

Do you see the pattern?

Different cultures, religions, time periods and all describing the same thing: intelligent beings from beyond Earth, flying vehicles, technology that seems divine, encounters both physical and spiritual.

And it's all in our sacred texts. We've had this information for thousands of years. We just never read it this way.

Maybe we focused so much on spiritual meaning that we missed the physical reality. Or maybe, and I believe this, it's both. Maybe the spiritual and physical aren't separate. Maybe these encounters were divine *because* they really happened.

Do you believe that angels, Jinn, Hindu deities, celestial beings, devas, all of these are part of the same phenomenon, just with different names based upon cultural context?

The ancient people back then did not have the word "alien." So when they saw beings coming from the sky, or from the "heavens", what else would they call them? They use words like divine, or angels or messengers of God.

But "heavens" is just another word for sky and for space.

Maybe God has been telling us about extraterrestrial life all along. Maybe these texts are both spiritual guides *and* historical records of real encounters.

And maybe that's exactly what God intended.

What Have We Learned?

We started with ancient civilizations leaving behind impossible structures and sudden advancements. Then we found sacred texts from multiple faiths describing beings from the heavens, advanced technology, and visitors bringing knowledge.

The thread runs through all of it.

We just never asked: what if they were describing something real?

Do you not believe that your faith expands if you believe that God's creation is much larger and much more wonderful than we previously imagined?

If Earth and humans have been visited throughout our

history then what does that mean for today?

It means the visits didn't stop.

So, What's Next?

Now it's time to fast-forward and travel through time again.

I believe that the visitations have been taking place throughout ancient times. Does that mean we are still being visited today?

The answer, as we'll see in the next section of this book, is a resounding F**K, YES!

But the encounters didn't stay in ancient deserts or in remote temples at the edge of the continent. They moved into the modern era. They started happening to trained military personnel like pilots and naval officers. It happened to people with radar systems and cameras and official documentation.

The visitors from above didn't disappear.

They started showing up in our skies during the time when we could photograph them and record them like never before.

When that happened, governments had a very clear choice to make. Should we tell the people the truth or shall we bury the truth? Can you take a wild guess at which one they chose? (Hint: not tell the truth.)

The following chapter is going to be a deeper dive into the more modern UFO phenomenon. We will be examining mass sightings and real documentation. It is going to explore the visitors popping up on military radar.

So, my dear Beautiful friend, please buckle up and hold tight. The sh*t is about to get very real!

CHAPTER 4

THEY NEVER STOPPED COMING

Alright, you Wonderful people. We have traveled through time through many different eras and seen a pattern emerge. We have found that there are visitors coming from the sky. There is advanced knowledge appearing out of nowhere. And there are encounters which defy logical explanation.

Some of you are probably thinking "Okay, okay, Mr B.

That's all really fascinating, bruh. But thousands of years ago, people were mad superstitious and stuff. They didn't understand science. Maybe they just saw natural phenomena and got freaked out AF."

That is a fair point and I get it. Ancient accounts can feel distant, maybe even questionable. Our ancestors didn't possess our technology or our scientific method, or even our skeptical mindset.

However, the point that I'm trying to get across to you now is that these visitations never stopped, not through the Middle ages or the Renaissance period or ever.

They... Never... Stopped!

What did change was our ability to document them. As humanity developed writing, printing presses, newspapers, and eventually cameras and radar, we got better at recording these events. The encounters became harder to dismiss as mere mythology or religious vision. There was better record-keeping.

And some of these documented sightings involved hundreds, sometimes thousands of witnesses. These are mass sightings. These events are so hugely public and undeniable that they make it into the official records and even into historical archives.

So, please allow me to take you through time once again. Now we come to a different era. We're going to look at some of the most incredible mass UFO sightings in recorded history. These events were witnessed by entire cities and documented by regular folks like you and I. That many people had absolutely nothing to gain and everything to lose by reporting what they saw.

We're going to start in the year 1561, in a German city, on

an April morning when the sky erupted into what can only be described as a battle. A battle in the skies over Nuremberg.

Get ready because this is where things start going insane!

April 4, 1561: The Battle Over Nuremberg

It is daybreak in Nuremberg, Germany on April 4th, the year fifteen sixty-one. The sun is just beginning to rise over the medieval city. People are waking up, starting their day, bakers are firing up their ovens, merchants preparing their stalls, and farmers heading to the fields for their harvest.

It's a normal morning, very quiet and peaceful.

And then the sky explodes with activity never witnessed before. The sky is suddenly filled with flying objects moving at tremendous speeds.

They were not birds or clouds. *Hundreds* of objects of various geometric shapes. Some were described as spheres, some were cylinders, and others crosses, moving at ridiculous speeds, weaving in and around each other, appearing to engage in some kind of an aerial combat. There was a battle in the sky that morning and people poured out of their homes, pointing up, shouting and yelling, some falling to their knees in prayer. The entire city is watching the event unfold.

This was really happening and it was bloody terrifying!

What They Saw In the Sky

There were detailed eyewitness accounts of what was seen that day and those accounts have been recorded and preserved. What we may call "cigar shaped craft" today were described as cylindrical objects in sky that day. What we may call "orbs" today were described as Red, blue and black spheres. These

UFOs weren't just floating around... oh no... they were moving rapidly. Zipping around the cylinders, darting between them, seemingly engaged in some sort of coordinated activity. WTH was going on?

Then there were crosses. Large cross-shaped objects that witnesses described with a mixture of religious awe and visceral fear. Were they interpreting the shapes through their religious world-view? Maybe. But they saw what they saw, and that was cross-shaped objects moving through the sky.

The weirdest part about it was that these objects appeared to be fighting each other in a battle.

Spheres would shoot toward other spheres. The cylinders seemed to be launching or controlling the smaller objects. This mass sighting took place for over an hour and witnesses even saw some objects colliding and crashing outside the city.

Over... An... Hour!

This wasn't a fleeting glimpse of something weird. No, sir. This was a sustained, prolonged event that the entire city witnessed together. When it finally ended, witnesses reported that the objects moved towards the sun and simply vanished. Just... disappeared.

The Documentation

The Nuremberg event is absolutely incredible from a historical standpoint. it was *documented*. Thoroughly and officially.

A printer and publisher named Hans Glaser created a broadsheet, basically a news poster, describing the event. He was a professional, a respected publisher, and he documented this event because it was newsworthy and because it happened.

Because an entire city had witnessed it and it was necessary that it be recorded and put on paper so that others would know about it.

The broadsheet still exists today. You can look at it. It's held in the Zentralbibliothek Zürich (Zurich Central Library) in Switzerland. The catalog number is PAS II 12/1563, if you want to verify this yourself. Here it is for your convenience:

The broadsheet includes a woodcut illustration showing the

objects in the sky. The cylinders, the spheres, the crosses, exactly as witnesses described them. And it includes text, a detailed written description of the event.

Let me share part of what that text says. This is a translation from the original German:

"In the morning of April 4, in the year 1561, at daybreak, between 4 and 5 a.m., a dreadful apparition occurred on the sun, and then this was seen in Nuremberg in the city, before the gates and in the country—by many men and women."

It goes on to describe the objects:

"At first there appeared in the middle of the sun two blood-red semi-circular arcs, just like the moon in its last quarter. And in the sun, above and below and on both sides, the color was blood, there stood a round ball of partly dull, partly black ferrous color... Likewise there stood on both sides and as a torus about the sun such blood-red ones and other balls in large number, about three in a line and four in a square, also some alone. In between these globes there were visible a few blood-red crosses."

The account continues, describing the aerial battle:

"Besides the globes and balls also saw a great number of big and small pipes... with these diverse objects... they all started to fight among themselves..."

And then the aftermath:

"After an hour or so, they all fell... from the sun and sky down to the earth, as if everything burned, and then it slowly faded on the earth with a lot of steam..."

The broadsheet concludes with the publisher noting that

God was showing people these signs as warnings, urging them to repent. That's the religious interpretation, and of course people in 1561 would interpret strange phenomena through a religious lens. That's all they had. It was normal back then to associate everything with God.

But strip away the religious interpretation and look at what's being described: multiple craft of different shapes, engaged in coordinated movement, appearing to battle each other, with some objects falling from the sky in flames.

Does that sound like a natural phenomenon to you? Like sun dogs or atmospheric reflections? How do atmospheric reflections battle each other for an hour?

Why This Matters

The Nuremberg event is significant for several reasons, and I want you to really think about this.

First: **Mass witnessing.** This wasn't one person claiming they saw something weird. This was an entire city. Hundreds or possibly thousands of people at once. Mass hallucination? Of the exact same complex event? For over an hour? Come on! Don't even get me started on that crap!

Second: **Contemporary documentation.** This was recorded when it happened, not decades later through oral tradition. Hans Glaser published this broadsheet within a couple of years of the event (the broadsheet is dated 1561, some sources say 1563, but either way, it's contemporary to the event). The witnesses were still alive. The memory was fresh. This wasn't mythology passed down through generations, this was news.

Third: **Detail and consistency.** The description is specific. Cylinders and spheres of specific colors. Cross shapes. Description of movement patterns and combat behavior.

Objects falling in flames. This level of detail doesn't come from vague impressions or misidentified natural phenomena. This comes from people describing what they actually saw.

Fourth: **No modern context for misidentification.** In 1561, there were definitely no airplanes, balloons, drones or military exercises. There were no fireworks displays that would look anything like this. People in 1561 knew what birds looked like. They knew clouds. They also knew celestial phenomena like eclipses and comets, but this was none of those things, and they knew it.

So what did they see?

I can't tell you for certain because I wasn't around. But I can tell you that whatever it was, it was real and it was physical. It scared the hell out of everyone who saw it. I know for a fact that I would be setting a new world record in sprinting if I watched UFOs battling it out over the skies of New York and New Jersey.

August 7, 1566: Basel, Switzerland—It Happens Again

More interesting stuff happened five years later in Europe.

August the 7th, fifteen sixty-six. The city of Basel, Switzerland. It's late afternoon, and the sky fills with strange objects.

This time, witnesses described large black spheres appearing near the sun, moving at high velocities. These spheres seemed to be fighting each other, just like in Nuremberg. They would turn red as if heated by their activity, and then many of them crashed to the ground, disappearing in smoke.

This event was also documented. Another broadsheet, another woodcut illustration, another written description. The

Basel broadsheet is held in the Wickiana Collection at the Zentralbibliothek Zürich (shelf mark PAS II 11/6). Here it is for your convenience, folks.

The text of the Basel broadsheet describes:

"At the time when the sun rose, one saw many large black balls which moved at high speed in the air towards the sun, then made half-turns, banging one against the others as if they were fighting a battle... and they became red and fiery, thereafter they were consumed and died out."

Black spheres... High speed... Combat behavior... Turning red and fiery... Eventually fading away.

Sound familiar don't it?

Two major European cities have mass sightings only five

years apart. Both experiencing objects in the sky engaging in what appeared to be aerial combat. Both events were documented in official publications. Both events were witnessed by hundreds maybe thousands of people.

What are the odds that these are unrelated coincidences? What are the odds that two separate cities, five years apart, just happened to experience the exact same type of mass hallucination or some misidentified natural phenomenon? Was everyone tripping? No. Most definitely not.

Or... how about this... what if something was *actually* happening? Perhaps these were not isolated incidents but rather a part of a much larger pattern of visitations that we're only now starting to recognize?

The 1800s: The Mystery Deepens

Let's fast foward to the 1800s. The Industrial Revolution is in full swing. Science is advancing rapidly. Newspapers are now everywhere and they report on current events with increasing detail.

The sightings continue.

Throughout the 19th century, there are scattered reports of strange objects in the sky. There are luminous objects... some cigar-shaped craft... other unexplained lights. Many go unreported or are dismissed, but then, in the late 1890s, something remarkable starts to happen.

America experiences what historians would later call "The Great Airship Wave."

Let's get into it.

1896-1897: The Great Airship Mystery

November 17, 1896. Sacramento, California. Evening. There is a large dark object moving in the sky against the wind and hundreds of people have reported it. The object has a bright searchlight beneath it.

Now, you might think: "Okay, dude, an airship. That makes sense, my bro. We had airships in the 1890s, n'est pas?"

Well... sort of. Experimental dirigibles existed, but they were primitive, unreliable, and certainly not capable of what people were reporting. And here's the thing: whatever these objects were, they showed up everywhere. Not just in California, but across the entire United States over the next eighteen months. Take a look at this:

Allow me to paint you a picture of what was happening.

The Wave Begins

After that initial sighting in Sacramento, reports started flooding Oakland, San Francisco, and San Jose. People across

California were seeing the same thing. It was a large, cigar-shaped craft, sometimes described as 150 feet long or more, moving through the night sky. It had lights, sometimes a powerful searchlight that would sweep the ground below, sometimes colored lights along its length. Some witnesses reported hearing mechanical sounds, like an engine or propellers.

This thing also moved *fast* and it moved against the wind. Witnesses watched it accelerate to speeds that no known airship could achieve. It would appear in one city, then hours later show up in another city hundreds of miles away. It seemed to be able to maneuver with precision, like making turns and adjustments that shouldn't be possible for a lighter-than-air craft.

By December 1896, the sightings had spread beyond California. Then, in early 1897, the phenomenon exploded across the Midwest and the rest of the country.

The Spread Across America

February through April 1897 was absolutely bonkers. Newspapers across the country were running daily stories about "the airship." People became obsessed. Reports from dozens of states were flooding in.

These reports were not "I saw a light in the sky" kinda reports. These were detailed accounts from credible witnesses including sheriffs, mayors, judges, businessmen, farmers, and even entire towns. People described the features of these craft with remarkable consistency.

Let me give you some specific examples that were reported in newspapers at the time:

Omaha, Nebraska—March 1897: The Omaha Daily Bee

reported that hundreds of people saw a large airship with a powerful light moving across the city. Witnesses included police officers as well as city officials. One witness described the object as a "cigar-shaped with wings" and said it moved "faster than any train."

Chicago, Illinois—April 10, 1897: Thousands of people in Chicago, IL reported seeing an airship. The Chicago Tribune covered the story extensively and they said witnesses described a cigar-shaped object with lights moving across Lake Michigan. One of the witnesses was a police officer and said he watched it through his binoculars and could even see "people moving around inside what appeared to be a cabin." Newspapers at the time weren't set up to publish photographs yet so they just did drawings of the photos. This is the published drawing of a photo:

Kansas City, Missouri—April 1897: The Kansas City Journal reported multiple sightings. This included one bizarre sighting where witnesses claimed to have actually met the pilots. Yes, you read that correctly, folks. Several people claimed they encountered the airship while it was on the ground and spoke to its occupants, who told them they were inventors testing a new flying machine. But when reporters tried to track down these inventors... they didn't exist. There were no names matched to any known inventors and no patents were filed. It was as if these "inventors" were just... stories. Do you think that something else was pretending to be a human inventor, perhaps?

And then there's my personal favorite incident because it's just so bizarre.

April 17, 1897: Aurora, Texas

Aurora, Texas. A tiny farming community with a small population of maybe 3000 people. It's totally not the type of place where you would expect international news to happen.

But on that one fine morning of April 17, eighteen ninety-seven, something crashed into a windmill on the property of Judge J.S. Proctor.

According to reports in the Dallas Morning News paper (dated April 19th 1897) published only two days after the incident, it said that an airship had been spotted traveling north over Texas and was moving slowly as if having mechanical issues. Once it was over Aurora, TX it apparently lost altitude completely and crashed into Judge Proctor's windmill. The crash destroyed both the Judge's windmill and the craft.

When townspeople gathered to examine the wreckage of the craft, they apparently found the body of the pilot. And according to the article, written by a local cotton buyer named S.E. Haydon, the pilot was "not of this world."

A Windmill Demolishes It.

Aurora, Wise Co., Tex., April 17.—(To The News)—About 6 o'clock this morning the early risers of Aurora were astonished at the sudden appearance of the airship which has been sailing through the country.

It was traveling due north, and much nearer the earth than ever before. Evidently some of the machinery was out of order, for it was making a speed of only ten or twelve miles an hour and gradually settling toward the earth. It sailed directly over the public square, and when it reached the north part of town collided with the tower of Judge Proctor's windmill and went to pieces with a terrific explosion, scattering debris over several acres of ground, wrecking the windmill and water tank and destroying the judge's flower garden.

The pilot of the ship is supposed to have been the only one on board, and while his remains are badly disfigured, enough of the original has been picked up to show that he was not an inhabitant of this world.

Mr. T. J. Weems, the United States signal service officer at this place and an authority on astronomy, gives it as his opinion that he was a native of the planet Mars.

Papers found on his person—evidently the record of his travels—are written in some unknown hieroglyphics, and can not be deciphered.

The ship was too badly wrecked to form any conclusion as to its construction or motive power. It was built of an unknown metal, resembling somewhat a mixture of aluminum and silver, and it must have weighed several tons.

The town is full of people to-day who are viewing the wreck and gathering specimens of the strange metal from the debris. The pilot's funeral will take place at noon to-morrow.   S. E. HAYDON.

The article states: *"The pilot of the ship is supposed to have been the only one aboard and, while his remains were badly disfigured, enough of the original has been picked up to show that he was not an inhabitant of this world."*

T.J. Weems, identified in the article as a Signal Service officer (basically, an Army weather observer) and "an authority on astronomy," reportedly examined papers found in the wreckage and said they were written in some form of hieroglyphics. He concluded that the pilot was probably "a native of the planet Mars."

Now, I know what you're thinking, you guys. This sounds insane. This sounds like the flippin' plot of a sci-fi movie. It is absolutely possible that S.E. Haydon made the entire incident up as a hoax to put Aurora, TX on the map or possibly just to have a little fun with the newspapers.

What we do know is that the article exists. It was published in a real newspaper. The town of Aurora exists. Judge Proctor was a real person. T.J. Weems was a real Signal Service officer stationed in nearby Fort Worth, TX and to this day there is a small metal marker in the Aurora cemetery which indicates an "unknown UFO pilot" is buried there. It was placed by the Aurora Historical Society.

Did all of this really happen? I honestly don't know the facts, because obviously I was not there. But to see such a story was actually published, in a legitimate newspaper, back in 1897, is remarkable in itself. At that time, the concept of aliens or ETs barely existed in popular culture. Legendary authors such as Jules Verne and H.G. Wells were just starting to write about space travel and the whole idea of beings from other planets was simply not yet a part of everyday conversation the way it might be today.

So if this was a hoax... well... it's really an ahead-of-its-time kinda hoax that introduced concepts most people wouldn't have even thought about. Would you agree?

And if it wasn't a hoax... well... What more can I say?

Why the Airship Wave Matters

The Great Airship Wave of 1896-1897 is significant for plenty of good reasons.

First, the sheer number of reports. We're talking about thousands of sightings over an 18-month period across most of the United States of America. So many newspapers covered these stories every single day. This was not some obscure type of phenomenon that only a few people knew about, this was show up as front-page news.

Second, the consistency of the descriptions. Cigar-shaped UFOs, large and fast-moving, big lights, especially searchlights, sometimes there were mechanical sounds, sometimes the occupants were described as human or human-like.

Third, and very importantly. Is the timing. These reports were happening before the Wright Brothers' first flight, which took place later in 1903. Before airplanes existed. Yes, experimental dirigibles and balloons existed, but nothing that could do what these airships were reported to do which was travel hundreds of miles in a night, move against strong winds, accelerate rapidly, maneuver with precision.

Skeptics say that the people were reporting experimental airships built by secret inventors who never came forward. I don't believe that for one second. The reason is that why would an inventor not come forward with his invention and capitalize on it. They could be world-famous and wealthy overnight! Secret inventors flying across the continent never patenting anything... that sounds harder to believe than actual UFOs if you ask me. The Wright brothers became famous instantly when they took their first flight. Also, the people who were seeing airships in the sky knew about airships, but the ones which were overhead in these reports behaved nothing like actual airships!

Sorry, but that simply doesn't make sense to me.

What makes more sense to me is that ordinary people saw something extraordinary and they reported it so that it gets recorded.

February 24-25, 1942: The Battle of Los Angeles

Alright, my Lovely friend. Let's take a quick leap in time to the 20th century. To World War II. This is a time when we had radar, anti-aircraft guns, searchlights, and also a military on high alert.

We will discuss an absolutely dramatic mass UFO sighting event where the United States military fired *over* 1,400 <u>anti-aircraft shells</u> at an unidentified object over Los Angeles, California, while thousands of civilians watched from the streets below.

This is Not ancient history. This isn't mythology. This is modern, documented, photographed military action against something in the sky.

The Setup

Let me set up the scenario for you, my friends. Let's visualize it. It's February of nineteen forty-two. Only two and a half months ago, on December 7 1941, Japan attacked America's Pearl Harbor base. The US of A is at war and on alert. Big time. The entire West Coast is on edge, terrified of another attack. Military installations are everywhere. Anti-aircraft batteries are strategically positioned throughout Los Angeles county. The residents are jumpy and nervous.

A false alarm is triggered on the evening of February 24.

There are reports of enemy aircraft approaching LA and air raid sirens sound. The city goes into blackout mode and the residents rush to their homes, close their curtains, turn off lights and go into hiding. Anti-aircraft crews man their positions while scanning the skies for enemy airplanes overhead.

But nothing happens. After a few tense hours, the all-clear is given and it was declared a false alarm. People breathe a sigh of relief and try to get some sleep.

But then... just after 3AM on February 25th... everything changes!

3:16 AM: The Object Appears

At 3:16AM, military radar picks up an unidentified flying object approaching at approximately 120 miles west of Los Angeles, California. It's moving towards the city!

This is not a drill or a false alarm like some hours ago. There is something on radar that's heading straight for one of America's largest cities... during wartime!! This is extremely serious!

Air raid sirens scream across Los Angeles, California and the city goes into full blackout. And this time, anti-aircraft crews don't wait. When the object gets close enough, they open fire. They unload.

Imagine if you were in Los Angeles that night. I mean you're already on edge from the earlier false alarm just hours ago and finally got to sleep. Then suddenly at 3am the sirens start again and shatter your peaceful slumber. You jump outta bed and look out the window where the sky is filled with searchlights pointed to the sky. Dozens of them sweeping back and forth across the darkness looking for something.

Then the guns start unloading their bullets... by the way I want to stress that these are ANTI AIRCRAFT SHELLS and they are made to pierce through metals and leave giant holes in their paths!!

The Attack

The 37th Coast Artillery Brigade, positioned throughout the Los Angeles area, begins firing. And they don't stop for over an hour. Over an HOUR!

Boom. Boom. Boom. Boom. Boom. Boom... etcetera.

Shell after shell after shell. The sound is deafening. The flashes from guns light up the night with explosions bursting in the sky as shells detonate. Shrapnel is raining down on to the city streets falling on roofs of homes and on the locals' cars.

All of this is aimed at... something up there?

The searchlights converge on a single point in the sky, and there, caught in the beams of light, is a flying object. There have been multiple witnesses who described it as a large, round or oval-shaped object which was Not like anything they've ever seen in their lives. It moves slowly and leisurely through the barrage of anti-aircraft fire.

The part that's hard to swallow is that this flying thing doesn't get damaged.

Shells are exploding all around it. Directly hitting it, according to some witnesses. But it doesn't fall or break apart. It doesn't seem affected at all. It just continues moving across the sky, drifting from Santa Monica to Long Beach, taking its sweet time. That's over 1400 <u>huge</u> shells that don't penetrate this object. How could this be any kind of conventional craft from an enemy nation?

The guns keep firing. That is 1430 rounds of anti-aircraft ammunition according to actual military reports. Think about that number. 1430 shells. That's not a brief skirmish. That's a sustained military engagement against something the United States Army cannot bring down despite their best efforts.

People are in the streets now, despite the air raid warnings. How could they not be? The noise, the lights, the explosions, it's totally impossible to ignore. Thousands of civilians watch this unfold. They see the searchlights holding an object in their beams. They see the explosions. They see this thing, whatever it is, moving through the barrage like it's nothing. You would be out watching it too, am I right?

And then around 4:15am it is all over. The object moves out of range, heading southeast. It disappears from radar. The guns fall silent and the searchlights go dark. The "all-clear" signal is given.

Los Angeles is left stunned and confused and trying to process what just happened.

The Evidence

Ladies and gentlemen, what I want you to be sure about is that this is not a myth or a legend. This is an actual documented military event with physical evidence. There are official records and photographic proof.

A photograph was published by the Los Angeles Times the following day which shows military searchlights converging on an unidentified flying object in the sky and also showing anti-aircraft bursts exploding all around it. That photograph still exists. You can look it up. It's one of the most famous UFO photographs in history, and it was taken during an actual military engagement. It's clearer online, but here it is:

This photograph shows the searchlights focusing on a single bright spot in the sky... please look closely at the point where all the lights meet... there is clearly something there because it is solid enough to reflect the searchlights. Again, it is a clearer image online. Something that was the target of sustained military fire and you can see the bursts of the artillery around it.

Military reports confirm the incident. The Thirty-Seventh Coast Artillery Brigade filed official documentation of the event and have even recorded the number of shells fired (officially 1,430), and the duration of the engagement (over one hour), along with the confirmation that no aircraft was shot down.

Casualty reports show that 5 civilians died that night. There were three from car accidents during the blackout and two from heart attacks, likely stress-induced by the chaos and fear. Also, there were numerous reports of property damage from falling shrapnel that went up had to come down, and pieces of exploded ordnance fell all over the city, damaging buildings and vehicles.

This was real. This happened. The physical evidence, damaged property, spent shell casings, the photograph, the official reports, all confirm it.

The Official Explanations (Or Lack Thereof)

So what did the military say they were shooting at? What exactly was their take?

Well, things start becoming messy from here.

Initially, Secretary of the Navy Frank Knox held a press conference on February 25 (the same day, just hours after the incident) and declared the whole thing was a "false alarm" caused by "war nerves." He essentially said that jittery anti-aircraft crews opened fire at nothing and got everyone else spooked. And the whole thing snowballed into mass hysteria.

But wait. If it was nothing, why did it show up on radar? Why did searchlights track a specific object for over an hour? Why did multiple independent witnesses describe seeing the same thing, a large, solid object in the sky? And how do you explain the photograph?

Secretary of War Henry Stimson contradicted Knox the very next day. On February 26, Stimson told reporters that the incident was *not* a false alarm. He said there were actually aircraft over Los Angeles, probably up to fifteen of them, and they were "unidentified."

Unidentified.

They were not Japanese or American. They were unidentified.

He suggested they might have been commercial planes operated by "enemy agents" trying to cause panic. But let us think about that for just a second. You wanna make me believe that enemy agents were flying commercial airplanes, slowly, vulnerably, and unarmed into the most heavily defended airspace on the West Coast of the USA... for what? Just to cause panic? And these planes survived **1,430 anti-aircraft shells** and just... flew away? And we never found them or caught the "enemy agents"? Anti-aircraft shells are made exactly for that reason, to successfully penetrate and destroy aircraft.

That explanation makes even less sense than Knox's "false alarm" story.

Later, in 1983, the U.S. Office of Air Force History conducted a review of the incident and concluded that it was most likely caused by a combination of "war nerves," weather balloons, and "unidentified aircraft."

Weather balloons. They went with the damn weather balloons excuse.

Weather balloons that appeared on radar, moved across the entire Los Angeles basin over the course of an hour, reflected searchlights brightly enough to be seen by thousands of people and photographed by the LA Times, and withstood 1,430 rounds of anti-aircraft fire without popping!!

Those are some seriously durable weather balloons, son! I swear I find this almost laughable.

So What Really Happened?

Look, I obviously can't tell you with 100% certainty what was in the sky over Los Angeles that night because nobody can. Whatever it was, it left. It didn't crash and no wreckage was recovered. No craft was captured.

But here's what we know for certain:

- Something showed up on radar.
- Something was tracked by searchlights for over an hour.
- The military fired 1,430 anti-aircraft shells at it.
- The object survived that barrage and moved away.
- Thousands of civilians witnessed it.
- It was photographed.
- The military's explanations contradict each other and don't make any sense.

So what does that leave us with?

An unidentified object. Literally unidentified, the military couldn't identify it, civilians couldn't identify it, and to this day, there's no satisfactory explanation that accounts for all the evidence.

Was it aliens in some advanced tech? I don't know... maybe. Was it something we still don't understand? Yes, probably.

But what I'm sure it absolutely, definitively was not is *nothing*. It wasn't war nerves. It wasn't weather balloons or mass hallucination. That is really preposterous.

Something was there. The United States military tried to shoot it down and failed. And then it just... left.

Oh and BTW, this was just one of many similar incidents

that would occur in the decades to come.

1946: Ghost Rockets of Scandinavia

Let's keep moving forward. The war is over now and the year is nineteen hundred and forty-six. Europe is recovering from the devastation of World War II. Out of nowhere in Scandinavia (Sweden, Norway, Finland) something very strange starts happening.

People start seeing rockets in the sky.

Lots of them. Starting with hundreds and then thousands!

The Wave Begins

The first reports come in May 1946, mostly from Finland. Witnesses describe seeing rocket-like objects streaking across the sky. They are moving at high speeds, sometimes leaving trails of smoke or fire behind them. At first, authorities assume these are Soviet missiles. Possibly leftover German V-2 rockets that the Soviets captured and might be testing.

But then the sightings explode in number. By June and July, Sweden is getting dozens of reports every day. Sometimes more than a hundred reports in a single day. People from all walks of life are seeing these things. This included farmers, to fishermen, to military personnel, to police officers, and even some scientists.

And the descriptions are *consistently* talking about "cigar-shaped" objects that are glowing and rocketing across the sky at immense speeds. Sometimes changing their direction and sometimes hovering. Here is a photo from 1946 published in a Swedish newspaper:

The Swedish military takes this seriously. Very seriously, in fact. They set up an official investigation, the Swedish Defense Staff's UFO investigation unit, and they dispatch military personnel to investigate crash sites.

Objects Crashing Into Lakes

Multiple witnesses reported seeing these "ghost rockets" crash into lakes. Not just small ponds, these are major lakes like Lake Kölmjärv and Lake Mjösa. There were dozens of reported crashes into water.

The military of Sweden sent out their best divers searching for a wreckage. They used the best possible equipment available to the government at the time, which included sonar equipment, advanced boats with equipment to scan the floor of the lake, searching for debris and evidence.

And they found... nothing.

No wreckage or debris. No impact craters on the lake bed. Nothing.

How does something solid enough to be seen, tracked visually by multiple witnesses, and reported as crashing into a lake just... vanish? Where did it go? How can it possibly disappear?

The Swedish military couldn't explain it. The official reports and documents by the Swedish military mention the complete absence of any physical evidence despite their searches. Now that's weird, dude!

Radar Tracking & Military Documentation

If you think this ended at visual sightings, well, then you're completely wrong. There were multiple Swedish radar stations tracking these objects. That includes radar operators and documented detections of objects that were moving very fast, matching the visual reports that came from civilians and military personnel alike.

The Swedish military had also created many detailed maps which show the flight paths of these objects. They were compiled by radar data and witness reports.

By the end of 1946, Sweden had received over 2,000 reports of ghost rockets. Two thousand! Damn! In less than a year. From a relatively small geographic area.

Norway and Finland reported hundreds more. That is pretty awesome stuff!

International Concern

This wasn't just a Swedish problem. The phenomenon was so widespread and so concerning that it became an international issue. The British and American governments took notice. The U.S. sent investigators to Sweden to study the reports and examine the evidence.

In October 1946, the Swedish military would hold a press conference acknowledging that most of the sightings were in fact genuine. That people were really seeing something unidentified. About 80% of the reports, they said, remained unexplained even after thorough investigation.

The Swedish Defense Staff's final report, declassified years later, concluded: "Most observations are clear, reliable and well documented. A considerable number of observations were made by trained and reliable observers... The descriptions are similar to each other and can hardly be explained as natural phenomena, Swedish or Russian missiles or imagination."

Read that again. The Swedish forces looked into it carefully and deeply, then said these things were real, not from nature, not made by Sweden nor Russia, and remained unexplainable.

What Were They?

The official Soviet response at the time was that these were not Soviet rockets. They denied any testing in Swedish airspace. Quite frankly, that denial actually makes sense. I mean why on Earth would the USSR risk international incidents by repeatedly firing missiles into neutral countries like Sweden and Norway? Let's say for sec that they were testing captured V-2 rockets... well, that doesn't explain the objects hovering or changing direction or crashing without leaving wreckage.

Some skeptics suggested the sightings might have been meteors. But meteors don't hover or change direction. They don't make multiple passes over the same area and they certainly don't crash into lakes without leaving any trace.

Others suggested secret military projects, maybe American or British technology being tested in Scandinavian airspace. But again, why? And how? What kind of tech back in 1946 could do what these objects reportedly did in the sky?

The ghost rockets of Scandinavia remain unexplained to this day. They remain one of the largest and most well-documented UFO waves in history. That includes thousands of reports, military investigations, radar tracking, and physical search operations, and yet, despite all this, not a single satisfactory conventional explanation has ever been provided by "the man".

1947: The Year Everything Changes

And now we arrive at 1947. This is *THE* year that would change everything. In 1947, UFOs, soon to be nicknamed "flying saucers", would burst into public view; people just couldn't look away. This moment sparked years of digging, speculating, controversies, and yet endless debate followed close behind.

We've seen it all before, it is a pattern. Nuremberg in 1561. Then Basel around 1566. Not long after, those airships popped up in America from 1896 into 1897. Fast forward to 1942 with LA's weird battle in the sky. Right behind that, Sweden got swarmed by ghost rockets in 1946.

The visitations never stopped. They evolved, they changed in character and frequency, but they never stopped.

And in 1947, everything came to a head. That's the year when a civilian pilot named Kenneth Arnold would see something that would create a new term which was "flying saucer." It was then that something smashed into the desert of New Mexico close to a small place named <u>Roswell</u> (ever heard of it?) setting off what'd become the biggest UFO event ever known. Around that time, the U.S. armed forces started their real, although messy and contradictory, role in the whole UFO business.

Before jumping into those key events, though, stop a sec. Think back on the CRAZY ride we've had so far.

Making Connections: From Ancient to Modern Skies

Think about where we started and where we are now.

We kicked things off with ancient civilizations who carved stories into rock, construction of impossible structures, and describing visitors from the sky. We explored sacred texts from the world's major religions which all seemingly contained references to beings from above, to encounters that sound technological.

There was no tech back then or any scientific method. There was no proper way to document what they were seeing except through art, architecture, and written word. We had to rely on their descriptions and their interpretations to try and make sense of something beyond their comprehension.

As we progress and evolve over the course of time, we begin to find better ways of recording.

By 1561, we had printing presses. Hans Glaser could create a broadsheet documenting the Nuremberg event and distribute it. The account was preserved, archived, made available for future generations to examine. We moved from oral tradition to documented history.

By the 1890s, we had newspapers everywhere. The Great Airship Wave wasn't just witnessed, it was reported daily, from coast to coast, in hundreds of publications. The Dallas Morning News published the Aurora, Texas story just two days after it allegedly happened. Documentation became immediate, widespread, and detailed.

By 1942, we had photography. The Los Angeles Times could capture the Battle of Los Angeles on film and publish it on the front page the very next day. We had radar detecting objects before they even became visible. We had military records documenting every shell fired, every minute of engagement. The evidence became tangible, physical, irrefutable.

By 1946, we had sophisticated military organizations conducting formal investigations. The Swedish Defense Staff didn't just dismiss the Ghost Rockets, they deployed teams, sent divers into lakes, tracked objects on radar, created detailed reports, and ultimately admitted they couldn't explain what was happening. Documentation became official, scientific, comprehensive.

Do you see the progression?

The phenomenon didn't change. The visitors didn't suddenly become more active or more visible. What changed was us. Our technology. Our ability to document, to verify, to prove that something real was happening.

And with that improved documentation came an unavoidable truth: this wasn't going away. This wasn't mythology or superstition or misidentification. Something's been flying in the sky, always present, ever since people first began gazing at the stars.

How We Got Here

Notice how responses to UFOs evolved over time? I mean just take a look at the pattern here. It will show you why government's involvement is the way it is.

1500s: Religious interpretations. "Signs from God."

1890s: Curiosity and mockery. No real investigation.

1942: Fear. The military fired 1,430 shells at something they couldn't bring down.

1946: Honest investigation. Sweden admitted: "We don't know what these are."

But here's what changed everything: the military got involved and realized they were powerless.

Ancient times? Ezekiel had his vision and that was it.

20th century? The military showed up with guns and radar. They fired, they searched and they investigated and they couldn't stop these things. That terrified them because governments exist to protect people. How do you stay safe from things you can't ID or control?

You cannot. Not honestly, at least. So you lie. You deny and you classify everything.

And that, my dear friends, is exactly what started in 1947.

What Comes Next

Everything we've covered, ancient accounts, religious texts, historical sightings, was leading here.

The ancient visitors became modern UFOs. Prophets became pilots. Sacred texts became classified files. But the phenomenon itself? It never changed or stopped.

1947 was when the cover-up and the big lies began.

Ready to see what happened at Roswell? Well, come on then!

CHAPTER 5

ROSWELL AND THE BIRTH OF DENIAL

Alright, everyone. We've reached the point that transformed everything. This was the year UFOs shifted from historical oddities to present-day emergencies. It was the year the military intervened like never before. The year the cover-ups genuinely started. By cover-up, I'm referring to the methodical and coordinated cover-up.

If you know the first thing about UFOs, well then you

definitely know this year to some extent. You heard the name Roswell before. It's directly connected to government conspiracy, with concealed facts, with extraterrestrials and cover-ups. However here's the astonishing part: the actual story is much more bizarre than the legends that have developed around it.

Firstly, what happened in '47 was not just a single occurrence. It was a surge. A series of reports across America that started in June and continued onwards. Then amid the chaos, an object crash landed in the New Mexico desert. The military announced they had recovered a "flying disc," and then, less than a day later, they changed their story.

That reversal? That twist? That instant flip of the original story? That is the moment when the denial started.

Lets break this down gradually. We'll review what actually occurred, what the eyewitnesses reported, what the military conveyed and identify the discrepancies that're so glaringly evident you can't help but wonder: what are they concealing?

June 24, 1947: The Sighting That Coined a Phenomenon

Before discussing Roswell, it's important that we talk about Kenneth Arnold. Because he's the one who sparked it all... at least in terms of the modern UFO era and the public consciousness of it.

June 24, 1947. Kenneth Arnold, a young 32-year-old businessman and seasoned pilot, is flying his CallAir A-2 near Mount Rainier in Washington State. He's engaged on a mission to search for a crashed C-46 Marine transport plane in the vicinity. The weather conditions are clear providing perfect visibility.

Then... he sees something moving.

Nine circular disc-shaped objects flying in formation near the peaks of the mountains. Their speed is fast, like *incredibly* fast. They are shiny objects and are reflecting the sunlight. Their flight pattern is unlike anything Arnold has experienced before.

So, Kenneth Arnold wasn't just some random dude making unfounded claims. He's an experienced aviator with over 9,000 hours of logged flight time. He's a businessman, a family man, a valued figure in his community. There was no benefit for him, yet everything to lose, by reporting a crazy claim like this. Yet what he witnessed was remarkable so unmistakable that he felt compelled to report it. It had to be documented.

When he lands in Yakima, Washington, he shares his sighting with other pilots. That same day upon arriving in Pendleton, Oregon he notifies the authorities and speaks with journalists, from the East Oregonian newspaper.

The Description

Allow me to share what Arnold reported in his own words.

Nine craft, flying in a diagonal, chain-like formation. They were moving from north to south along the Cascade mountain range. Each craft was disc-shaped, flat, reflective—like "a saucer would if you skipped it across water." That's the expression he used and that is where we got the term "flying saucer."

Here is a photo of Kenneth Arnold holding up an artist's sketch/rendering of his description.

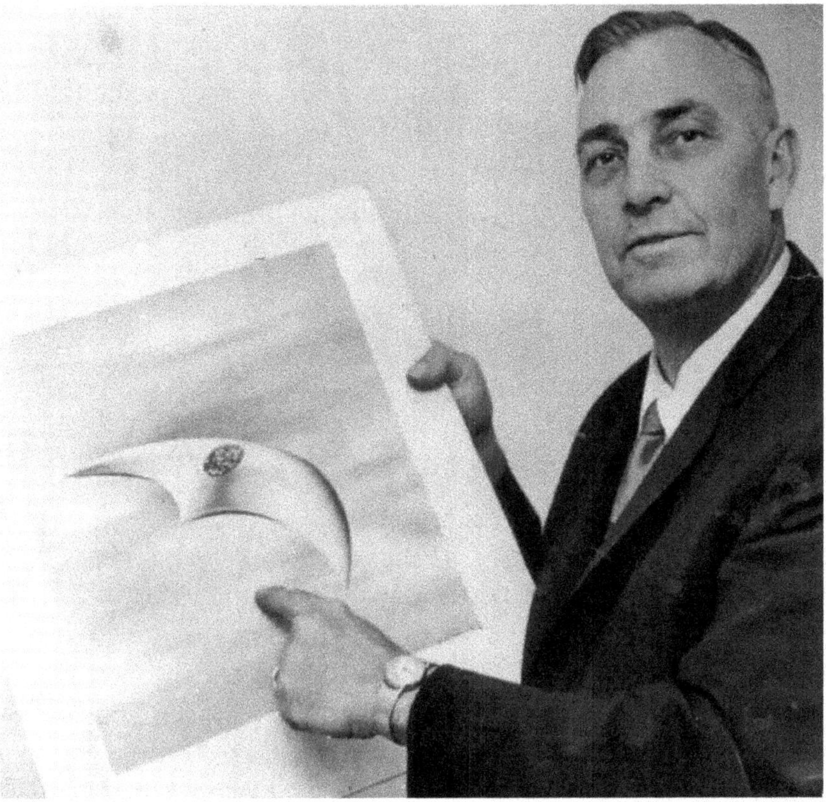

More importantly, Arnold was able to calculate their velocity.

He timed them. He watched them move between Mt. Rainier and Mt. Adams which was a distance he knew. He calculated their speed at roughly 1700 miles per hour. Just FYI in 1947 the fastest aircraft in the world, the experimental Bell X-1, hadn't even broken the sound barrier yet (that would happen later that year in October, reaching 700 mph). Commercial & military aircraft flew at maybe 400-500 mph max.

Arnold observed these objects move at 1,700 mph. That was more than three times faster than anything humans had constructed back then.

He reported this to the Army Air Forces because he felt like they should be aware. They regarded his account with importance. Hours later, his narrative had gotten to the newspapers. When the media got a hold of this story... Ooohhhh Mama!

The Explosion

The East Oregonian published Arnold's story the very next day on June 25, 1947. The headline read: "Impossible! Maybe, But Seein' Is Believin', Says Flyer."

That was the moment the story just exploded!

Newspapers nationwide picked up the story. "Flying saucers" became a universal term. Suddenly, reports started pouring in from all over the place. People who had seen strange things in the sky but never reported them now felt encouraged to come forward. New sightings were reported daily.

In the coming weeks, hundreds of sightings would be reported across the US of A. Pilots, civilians, cops and all sorts of people shared their observations. They all reported objects moving at insane speeds and performing maneuvers that contradicted the laws of physics.

Kenneth Arnold's sighting opened the floodgates. It triggered a surge of reports... and the military was watching. They were investigating and treating this issue with importance.

But publicly? They were about to start lying. Like big time!

July 1947: UFO Crashes in Roswell

Roughly two weeks after Kenneth Arnold's sighting,

something happened in the desert outside Roswell, New Mexico that would become the most renowned UFO case in history.

We know it happened because of the existing documentation. We have multiple witnesses as well as the military's own press release. The truth we don't have is what actually crashed.

Let me walk you through it, one piece at a time, and you decide if the official account holds up.

Early July 1947: The Crash

It's the second or third of July 1947. There's stormy weather over the New Mexico desert. An explosive crashing sound is heard by rancher Mac Brazel, who manages the Foster Ranch approx 75 miles northwest of Roswell.

The next morning, he goes out to check on his sheep. That's when he finds it.

Debris. A lot of debris scattered across a large area of his property, some reports say the debris field was three-quarters of a mile long and several hundred feet wide. This isn't just a small amount of wreckage. This is pretty damn substantial.

And it's unlike anything Brazel has ever seen.

The Debris: What Was It?

Things continue getting more interesting. Mac Brazel has seen weather balloons before. He's found debris from them on his property previously. He knows what they look like and according to him, this wasn't that.

Here's what he and other witnesses described finding:

Strange metallic material: Unusual metallic substance: Slim, light, bendable, yet remarkably durable. Observers claimed it was impossible to slice, burn or rip. If you balled it up it would straighten out on its own. Revert to its pristine smooth form. It refused to have any folds or creases.

I-beams: Small structural pieces, lightweight like balsa wood but incredibly strong. The kicker? They had markings on them looking like hieroglyphics or some unknown writing system. Purple/Pink in color.

Foil-like material: Reflective, thin as paper, but you couldn't puncture it or damage it. Some witnesses compared it to aluminum foil, except it was far stronger and had that strange "memory" property where it would return to shape.

No conventional components: No wires, no electronics, no engines, no fuel, nothing that looked like it came from any known aircraft or balloon.

Mac Brazel was puzzled. He discussed it with his neighbors. Ultimately he chose to notify the authorities.

On July 6th 1947 he went to Roswell and informed Sheriff George Wilcox about the wreckage. Sheriff Wilcox promptly reached out to Roswell Army Air Field, home to the 509th Bomb Group, the only atomic bomb squadron in the world at that time. This was a secured military facility. They treated the report with total seriousness.

July 6-7: The Military Steps In

Major Jesse Marcel, the intelligence officer at Roswell Army Air Field, was sent out to investigate the crash along with Captain Sheridan Cavitt from the Counter Intelligence Corps.

Now, let's take a pause over here. Major Jesse Marcel wasn't just a low-level soldier. He was the intelligence officer for the 509th. For those of you who don't know, that is the unit that had dropped the atomic bombs on Japan just two years earlier. He was trained to identify aircraft, recognize enemy technologies, and assess all manners of threats. He was knowledgeable, experienced, and credible.

Marcel and Cavitt went to the ranch. They examined the wreckage and loaded up the fragments into their vehicles. Marcel later stopped by his home on the way back to the base to show his wife and son. He was excited. He told them, "This is something I've never seen before. This is not from Earth."

His son, Jesse Marcel Jr., only 11 years old, later recounted dealing with the I-beams marked with unusual symbols. He recalled the material that was impervious to damage. He also remembered his fathers enthusiasm and firm belief that this was something extraordinary.

Marcel brought the debris back to Roswell Army Air Field. It was examined. It was forwarded through the chain of command. Then on July 8th 1947 an event, unlike any occurred.

An announcement was made by the military.

July 8, 1947: "RAAF Captures Flying Saucer"

This is the part where things go nuts, and it's documented. It is not speculation nor is it conspiracy theory. It's a historical fact.

On July 8, 1947, Lt. Walter Haut was a public information officer at Roswell Army Air Field. He issued an official press release on behalf of the 509th Bomb Group. It was sent to the local newspapers and radio stations.

I'm going to quote directly from the Roswell Daily Record, which published it on the same day:

"The many rumors regarding the flying disc became a reality yesterday when the intelligence office of the 509th Bomb Group of the Eighth Air Force, Roswell Army Air Field, was fortunate enough to gain possession of a disc through the cooperation of one of the local ranchers and the sheriff's office of Chaves County."

Read that again. "The intelligence office... was fortunate enough to gain possession of a disc."

A disc. Not a weather balloon. A disc.

The press release continued:

"The flying object landed on a ranch near Roswell sometime last week. Not having phone facilities, the rancher stored the disc until such time as he was able to contact the sheriff's office, *who in turn notified Maj. Jesse A. Marcel of the 509th Bomb Group Intelligence Office."*

This was an official military press release from a major Army Air Field. They announced they had recovered a flying disc.

The Roswell Daily Record had it front page with the following headline: "RAAF Captures Flying Saucer On Ranch in Roswell Region."

Radio stations broadcast the news. Other newspapers picked it up and for a few hours, it was the biggest story in US.

And then came an important turning point. Yes, this is the big one!

July 9, 1947: The Reversal

Less than 24 hours later, literally the very next day, the story had somehow completely flipped a complete 180 degrees.

Brigadier General Roger Ramey, commander of the Eighth Air Force at Fort Worth Army Air Field in Texas, called together a press conference. Major Jesse Marcel was there, standing next to a pile of debris laid out on the floor.

And General Ramey announced: it wasn't a flying disc. *It was a weather balloon.*

Just a regular weather balloon with a radar reflector. Nothing extraordinary or alien. It was just a mundane weather device that Mac Brazel and Major Marcel who were both experienced men, one a rancher who'd seen weather balloons before, the other an intelligence officer trained to identify aircraft, had somehow misidentified.

The press photographed Marcel with the weather balloon

debris. Those photos still exist. And if you look at them, you'll notice something: the debris in the photos looks like a weather balloon. Some torn rubber, little balsa wood, some foil. Standard stuff.

But here's the question: is that the same debris Marcel collected from the ranch?

Marcel himself, in interviews decades later, said absolutely not. He said the weather balloon in those photos was a substitution. He said, "That's not the stuff I brought in. That's not what we found."

The official story became: weather balloon. Case closed. Nothing to see here. Keep it movin', folks!

And Mac Brazel? After making his initial report, he was held by the military for several days. When he eventually spoke to the media again his demeanor had changed. He appeared reserved and hesitant to discuss the matter. He informed the Roswell Daily Record that he regretted reporting it in the first place as it had created excessive problems.

Whatever happened to him during military custody changed his story and his demeanor.

The Witnesses: Their Perspective?

Since 1947 researchers have spoken with several individuals connected to the Roswell incident, whether directly or indirectly. A large number of these discussions took place between the 1970s and 1990s so naturally memories dulled and some specifics could be uncertain. Nevertheless the uniformity of the testimonies is remarkable.

Here are a few key testimonies:

Major Jesse Marcel:

Before he died in 1986. Marcel was adamant about what he had found. It was Not a weather balloon. He had given interviews in the late 70s and 80s and recalled the material as being extremely durable light in weight and bearing unusual symbols. He claimed that the military hid the truth, that he was instructed to support the weather balloon cover-up and that he wished he had spoken out earlier.

Mac Brazel's son, Bill Brazel Jr.: The son had helped his father gather up some of the debris before the military arrived on scene. He described the same characteristics: metallic material that couldn't be cut or burned, foil that returned to shape, small I-beams with strange markings.

Loretta Proctor: This was a neighbor of Mac Brazel and he had brought a piece of the debris to her house before reporting it. She described it as "like thin aluminum foil, but you couldn't cut it, couldn't tear it." She said Mac was genuinely baffled by it.

Glenn Dennis: A mortician based in Roswell who claimed that the military contacted his funeral home asking about small, child-sized coffins. He further claimed that a nurse friend at the base told him about strange bodies being examined. His testimony is controversial because some details don't check out, but the coffin inquiry is peculiarly specific.

Lieutenant Walter Haut: This was the public information officer who issued the original "flying disc" press release. In a signed affidavit made public after his demise in 2005, Haut stated that he was shown the actual craft stored in a hangar at the base. He said it was Not weather balloon. He said he knew the weather balloon story was a cover-up.

Brigadier General Thomas DuBose: This was the Chief of Staff to General Ramey in 1947. During an invterview in 1991, Brig Gen DuBose admitted that the weather balloon story was indeed fabricated. He said the debris was flown into Washington for a high-level examination and according to him the cover story was ordered from "way up at the top."

Can you notice the pattern here? Several witnesses, numerous of whom are military members, with no motive to fabricate their stories. They all report the same claim: that the official account was false.

The Official Story Evolves (Yet Again)

At this point you may be wondering: "Alright, yo! But surely the military provided an explanation eventually? It's been years. They must have revealed the events by now?" "

Well, they tried. And it's almost more suspicious than the original cover-up.

Forty-seven years after the Roswell incident, the US Air Force released a report in 1994 titled: "The Roswell Report: Fact vs. Fiction in the New Mexico Desert." This report claimed that the debris was actually from Project Mogul, a top-secret program using high-altitude balloons to detect nuclear tests conducted by the USSR.

Okay well that's at least more intriguing than "weather balloon." Project Mogul was a classified program involving balloons.

But here's the problem: even if it was Project Mogul, that doesn't explain the witness descriptions. Project Mogul balloons were made of regular rubber and radar reflectors made of balsa wood and foil. They were not indestructible They lacked hieroglyphic markings and didn't regain their shape after being crumpled.

How could Major Marcel, an intelligence expert skilled in identifying aircraft and technology, misidentify a balloon as something extraterrestrial? Why would the military release a statement claiming they had retrieved a "disc" if they were aware it was a balloon operation? Wouldn't they simply remain silent about it because it's supposed to be classified?

Subsequently in 1997 the Air Force published a document called "The Roswell Report: Case Closed" which sought to clarify the "alien bodies" that some observers reported to have seen. They clarified that these were in fact crash test mannequins utilized in high-altitude parachute trials during the 1950s.

Wait. The 1950s? The Roswell incident took place in 1947. The Air Force was suggesting that witnesses confused events from different decades?

That's... not great.

Let me get this straight. Official explanations went from "weather balloon" to a "secret spy balloon" to "crash test dummies" from 10 years later. The story continued changing, but the fundamental questions remained unanswered.

So WTF Happened at Roswell?

Look, I cannot tell you what crashed in Roswell because I was not there.

But I can tell you what's really suspicious sounding:

- **The military announced they recovered a "flying disc"** in an official press release.
- **They reversed that story within 24 hours** and have stuck with variations of "it was a balloon" ever since.
- **Multiple witnesses,** including military personnel with high security clearances, have said the official story is false.
- **The debris descriptions** do not match any known tech from 1947 or even today.
- **The official explanation has changed numerous times** and every version turning more and more elaborate than the previous.
- **The hyper level of security and confidentiality** applied to what was supposedly just a weather balloon is purely bizarre stuff. Why threaten witnesses or seize the wreckage? Why classify and keep things under wraps for a damn balloon?

Something happened at Roswell. Something that was significant enough for the military to announce it publicly and then immediately try to bury it. Something that frightened them to keep it classified for over 75 years.

Could it be an alien spacecraft? I dunno. But it's something they do not want the public to know about.

And Roswell was not an isolated incident. It was the moment when the pattern of denial truly started taking shape.

September 1947: Project Sign and the Birth of Systematic Denial

Just two months after Roswell, two months after Kenneth Arnold, after the wave of sightings, after the crash and the cover-up—the U.S. Air Force established Project Sign.

This was the first official military program tasked with investigating UFO reports. And at first, they actually took it seriously. The government obviously believes in UFOs to be able to start investigating them. I mean, YOU (yes, you the reader) wouldn't investigate unicorns if you didn't believe they exist, right?

Project Sign: The Honest Investigation

Project Sign consisted of scientists, engineers and military intelligence personnel. Their responsibility was to gather reports examine information and identify the nature of these "flying saucers."

Remarkably, they did their job honestly. They investigated and they interviewed witnesses. They examined evidence and they came to a conclusion.

In 1948 Project Sign produced a classified report called the "Estimate of the Situation" which went up the chain of command to the highest levels of the Air Force.

What was the conclusion of this document?

That UFOs were real. That they were not U.S. aircraft, not Soviet aircraft, and not natural phenomena. And that the most likely explanation was that they were extraterrestrial in origin.

The people investigating UFOs for the military, those trained professionals with access to all the reports and all the classified data, concluded that we were being visited by extraterrestrial craft.

How did the Air Force respond?

The Rejection

General Hoyt Vandenberg, Chief of Staff of the Air Force, rejected the "Estimate of the Situation." It was not because the evidence was weak or that the analysis was flawed or because the conclusion was unacceptable.

He ordered the document destroyed... literally destroyed. Every copy was supposed to be burned.

Why? Because you cannot inform your people or the global community that alien vehicles are navigating our skies. You cannot admit that you cannot control or intercept them or understand how they operate.

You cannot admit how powerless you are. That would mean weakness.

So instead, the Air Force shifted gears.

Project Grudge: The Debunking Mission

In 1949, Project Sign was renamed as Project Grudge. If that name isn't a dead give-away, then let me spell it out: the mission changed from investigation to debunking.

Project Grudge's job wasn't to find the truth. It was to explain away UFO sightings by any means necessary. It was to ridicule and to make a mockery of the topic. Weather balloons, the planet Venus, swamp gas, mass hallucinations, hoaxes... any rationale or justification was acceptable as long as it excluded the words "extraterrestrial craft."

Captain Edward Ruppelt, who subsequently led the successor initiative Project Blue Book discussed this in his 1956 publication "The Report, on Flying Objects." He verified that the "Estimate of the Situation" was real and that it determined UFOs were extraterrestrial. He also confirmed that it was rejected and destroyed.

Ruppelt wrote: "The situation was being 'estimated' as being real; the objects were interplanetary."

But that reality was deemed too dangerous to acknowledge.

So instead, the Air Force adopted a policy that would persist for decades going forward: investigate privately, deny publicly. Collect reports, analyze data, brief the higher-ups, but tell the public nothing. Or worse, tell them it's all nonsense. Tell them it's just swamp gas or something else ridiculous.

The Pattern Established

And that's how the systematic denial began.

1947 set the template:

- Something extraordinary happens
- The military investigates
- The evidence points to something unknown, possibly extraterrestrial
- The official response is denial and cover-up
- Witnesses are discredited
- Evidence is classified or destroyed
- The public is told nothing, or they're told lies

This pattern would repeat itself over and over again for the next 70+ years. We'll see it with countless other cases. We'll see it with gov't programs which officially "do not exist." We'll see it with whistleblowers who risk everything to tell the truth then only to be dismissed or ridiculed.

But it all started here. In 1947. With Roswell and the birth of denial. Now there was a system in place to handle it. To contain it and to keep the public in the dark.

What Comes Next

We've seen the pattern established. We've seen the birth of denial. We have seen how 1947 changed everything.

Now, in the next chapter, we will leap ahead to explore subsequent events. We will review some of the intriguing and thoroughly recorded UFO sightings from more recent years. Instances featuring eyewitness accounts, radar evidence, video recordings and official documentation.

We are going to see that the phenomenon didn't fade away but rather became more frequent and more brazen.

We will review pilots pursuing targets that surpass everything in our military arsenal. We'll examine the famous "Tic Tac incident" from 2004 that was captured on Navy infrared cameras. We will explore how these encounters have been documented, studied, and then... surprise, surprise... classified and buried!

Because the pattern that started in 1947 persists even today.

There are some differences, however, and the truth is slowly coming out. Classified documents are now being declassified. Whistleblowers are speaking out more, and the Pentagon has admitted that UAPs (previously known as flying discs or UFOs) are real and that they don't know what they are.

We're living through the early stages of disclosure. Their decades of denial is breaking and the truth is emerging.

But to understand how we got here, we needed to understand where it all began and that is why we needed to review Roswell. We needed to see the birth of denial.

Now, my Wonderful friend, let us discover what they've been hiding all these years.

Let's look at the modern encounters... I mean the ones which they cannot explain away, no matter how hard they try!

Ready? Here we go!

CHAPTER 6

MODERN ERA ENCOUNTERS

So, just to summarize, we've established the pattern. We've seen how it started in Roswell, NM in 1947. The military's announcement of a "flying disc," followed immediately by complete denial. Project Sign's honest conclusion that UFOs were extraterrestrial, rejected and destroyed. The shift to Project Grudge and the birth of systematic debunking. How wonderful!

The pattern was set: investigate privately, deny publicly.

Repeat. Continue doing this.

The problem with patterns is they're hard to maintain when the evidence keeps piling up. When witnesses keep coming forward and technology advances to the point where you can't just dismiss sightings as "weather balloons" or "swamp gas" anymore.

Because now we have radar, infrared cameras, multiple sensor systems on military aircraft. We have sophisticated tracking equipment. We also have high-definition video. And most importantly, we have trained military observers such as pilots, radar operators, intelligence officers, who know what they're looking at and aren't afraid to document it. They are a very integral part of the story and the path towards disclosure.

The phenomenon did not stop after 1947, au contraire mes amis, it intensified. As our technology improved, so did our documentation. The encounters grew more difficult to ignore, tougher to rationalize and more challenging to hide beneath layers of confidentiality and media distortion.

This chapter will guide us through some of the compelling UFO sightings from modern times. Instances involving witnesses, physical evidence, radar confirmation, recorded videos and official documentation. Cases documented so comprehensively and examined so meticulously that the that the only way to dismiss them is to ignore them entirely.

We are going to be seeing how each of these cases slowly chipped away to crack their barrier of denial. How they built pressure and forced conversations. How they paved the way for what's happening right now... official disclosure.

Are you amped? Because some of these stories are truly unbelievable!

December 26-28, 1980: The Rendlesham Forest Incident

Let me take you to England, United Kingdom. It's December 1980, Cold War era. It's December 1980 during the Cold War period. RAF Woodbridge, a Royal Air Force station located in Suffolk is operated in partnership, with the United States Air Force. This NATO installation houses nuclear weapons, so obviously security is set to the max! The personnel are trained, professional, perpetually on high alert. There are no untrained professionals at these types of facilities, especially facilities which are jointly affiliated by the USA and the UK, both major power-houses.

It's the day after Christmas... December 26, 1980, just past midnight. Two USAF security policemen, Airman John Burroughs and Airman Edward Cabansag are patrolling the forest outside the base perimeter. They suddenly see some strange lights descending into the trees. The lights are multi-colored and moving and are nothing like aircraft lights.

At first, they think it might be a downed plane. They call it in. Staff Sergeant Jim Penniston, the security officer on shift is sent out to check it along with them.

What follows is one of the most well-documented and most credible UFO encounters in history.

Night One: The Encounter

Penniston, Burroughs, and Cabansag make their way through Rendlesham Forest toward the lights. It's dark, it's foggy, and the trees are dense. As they get closer, they realize this isn't a plane crash at all. This is some other object.

It's some kind of craft and it's sitting in a small clearing.

Penniston would later describe it in incredible detail.

It was triangular, 9 feet in length and 6.5 feet in height. The object appeared dark, metallic and sleek without any joints, bolts or obvious means of propulsion. There are symbols on its surface like strange glyphs, etched or raised, running along one side. They look almost hieroglyphic. It does not resemble any language or alphabet currently known on Earth.

The craft is hovering a foot off the ground. A strong white glow is radiating from it. The atmosphere nearby feels unusual and the air is buzzing with electricity causing the hairs on their arms to rise.

Penniston approaches. He's a trained security officer, BTW. His job is to investigate, to document, and to evaluate dangers. So he does what he's trained to do: he gets real close. He examines it and reaches out and touches it.

The surface is smooth, warm, like glass but not quite. And as he touches it, he gets the overwhelming sense that this thing is... alive or aware? He can't quite explain it, but it feels like it's responding to him.

He takes out his notebook. He sketches what he sees. He writes down descriptions. He notes the symbols and the dimensions, everything he can observe. This is currently an official military investigation in progress, and he's documenting it like the way he has been trained.

Burroughs circles around the object to get a full view. Cabansag hangs back, radioing reports to the base. Suddenly, the craft begins to move.

The object hovers higher off the ground and its light intensifies. In a sudden instant, faster than anything they have ever seen, it shoots upwards through the trees and disappears into the sky like it was never even there.

There is no exhaust, or sound, or explanation.

The three men stand there in stunned silence. WTH did they just see? What the heck was parked near a secure nuclear military base?

The Physical Evidence

What makes Rendlesham different from a lot of UFO cases is that they had physical evidence.

The following morning armed forces went back to the location. They discovered three indentations in the earth arranged in a triangular shape, exactly where Penniston had indicated the craft was. Each indentation measured 7 inches across and 1.5 inches deep as if a heavy object had been resting there.

They took soil samples. They took radiation readings. And those readings were elevated. Were they dangerously dangerously high? No, but significantly above background levels. Something had been there and that something left measurable traces enough to confirm it was there.

Night Two: Lt. Col. Halt Takes Over

A couple of nights later, on December 28, 1980, unusual lights are reported once again in the forest. By then, news of what Penniston and his group experienced has circulated throughout the base. So when the reports come in, the Deputy Base Commander, Lieutenant Colonel Charles Halt, decides he's going to investigate this himself to see what's up.

Halt is not some junior enlisted guy. He's a high ranking officer, a seasoned military professional, someone experienced in battle a no-nonsense kinda person. He gathers a team to go into the forest with him to find out what's really going on.

He brings measuring equipment like a radiation detector. And critically, this is so important, he brings a portable cassette recorder and documents everything in real time.

That recording still exists. You can listen to it. It is publicly available. It's Halt and his team, in the forest, reacting to what they're seeing as it happens. No memory reconstruction decades later. This is live audio from the moment and you can find it online. The man sounds absolutely horrified as he approaches the craft. Check it out, please!

The Halt Memo

Let's move to the crucial evidence: on January 13 1981, merely weeks following the event Lt. Col. Halt composed an official memorandum addressed to the UK Ministry of Defense (The MOD). This document, named "Unexplained Lights," describes the encounters in detail. It is a official military document filed through proper channels documenting UFO activity at the NATO base.

Let me quote parts of it:

"Early in the morning of 27 Dec 80 (approximately 0300L), two USAF security police patrolmen saw unusual lights outside the back gate at RAF Woodbridge. Thinking an aircraft might have crashed or been forced down, they called for permission to go outside the gate to investigate. The on-duty flight chief responded and allowed three patrolmen to proceed on foot..."

It continues:

"The individuals reported seeing a strange glowing object in the forest. The object was described as being metallic in

appearance and triangular in shape, approximately two to three meters across the base and approximately two meters high. It illuminated the entire forest with a white light. The object itself had a pulsing red light on top and a bank(s) of blue lights underneath. The object was hovering or on legs. As the patrolmen approached the object, it maneuvered through the trees and disappeared..."

And then, about his own investigation on the 28th:

"*Later in the night a red sun-like light was seen through the trees... At one point it appeared to throw off glowing particles and then broke into five separate white objects and then disappeared. Immediately thereafter, three star-like objects were noticed in the sky... The objects moved rapidly in sharp angular movements and displayed red, green and blue lights...*"

He documents the radiation readings: "*Beta/gamma readings of 0.1 milliroentgens were recorded with peak readings in the three depressions and near the center of the triangle formed by the depressions. A nearby tree had moderate (.05-.07) readings on the side of the tree toward the depressions.*"

This is an official military memo written by a Deputy Base Commander describing UFO activity and documenting physical evidence. It was submitted through proper channels. Here it is for your convenience.

DEPARTMENT OF THE AIR FORCE
HEADQUARTERS 81ST COMBAT SUPPORT GROUP (USAFE)
APO NEW YORK 09755

REPLY TO
ATTN OF: CD   13 Jan 81

SUBJECT: Unexplained Lights

TO: RAF/CC

1. Early in the morning of 27 Dec 80 (approximately 0300L), two USAF security police patrolmen saw unusual lights outside the back gate at RAF Woodbridge. Thinking an aircraft might have crashed or been forced down, they called for permission to go outside the gate to investigate. The on-duty flight chief responded and allowed three patrolmen to proceed on foot. The individuals reported seeing a strange glowing object in the forest. The object was described as being metalic in appearance and triangular in shape, approximately two to three meters across the base and approximately two meters high. It illuminated the entire forest with a white light. The object itself had a pulsing red light on top and a bank(s) of blue lights underneath. The object was hovering or on legs. As the patrolmen approached the object, it maneuvered through the trees and disappeared. At this time the animals on a nearby farm went into a frenzy. The object was briefly sighted approximately an hour later near the back gate.

2. The next day, three depressions 1 1/2" deep and 7" in diameter were found where the object had been sighted on the ground. The following night (29 Dec 80) the area was checked for radiation. Beta/gamma readings of 0.1 milliroentgens were recorded with peak readings in the three depressions and near the center of the triangle formed by the depressions. A nearby tree had moderate (.05-.07) readings on the side of the tree toward the depressions.

3. Later in the night a red sun-like light was seen through the trees. It moved about and pulsed. At one point it appeared to throw off glowing particles and then broke into five separate white objects and then disappeared. Immediately thereafter, three star-like objects were noticed in the sky, two objects to the north and one to the south, all of which were about 10° off the horizon. The objects moved rapidly in sharp angular movements and displayed red, green and blue lights. The objects to the north appeared to be elliptical through an 8-12 power lens. They then turned to full circles. The objects to the north remained in the sky for an hour or more. The object to the south was visible for two or three hours and beamed down a stream of light from time to time. Numerous individuals, including the undersigned, witnessed the activities in paragraphs 2 and 3.

CHARLES I. HALT, Lt Col, USAF
Deputy Base Commander

And how did the UK Ministry of Defense respond? They said it was "of no defense significance."

Sure! Right! Okay, bruh! An unknown craft landing at a NATO nuclear weapons facility is of no defense significance. Sure. I believe that. I'm so gullible and love believing any old BS.

PS: *I'm being f**king sarcastic.*

Why Rendlesham Matters

The Rendlesham Forest incident is frequently referred to as "Britain's Roswell," and for good reason. You have:

- Multiple trained military witnesses
- Physical trace evidence (ground depressions, radiation readings)
- Real-time audio documentation
- An official military memo submitted through proper channels
- Witness testimonies that have remained consistent for over 40 years

Penniston, Burroughs, and Halt have all spoken publicly about what they saw. They've testified and they've been interviewed extensively. Their stories haven't changed. They've faced ridicule, skepticism, and career damage for speaking out, but they've stuck to their accounts because they know what they experienced.

In 2001 and 2007 the UK government published thousands of pages of documents relating to UFOs. Included were the Rendlesham files, which confirmed that this inquiry did actually take place and that the memo is authentic. That the military regarded it seriously despite the official stance being one of dismissal. That's just amazing ain't it!?

Rendlesham showed that the phenomenon wasn't just an American issue. It was happening to NATO allies. It was happening at high-security installations. And it was being documented by credible, trained observers.

Despite the continuation of denial, the cracks were starting to show.

November 17, 1986: Japan Airlines Flight JAL 1628

Jumping forward six years and across the Pacific ocean. We find ourselves in frigid Alaskan airspace now, 35,000 feet above the frozen expanse. The time is now 5pm on November 17, 1986. It is cold with perfect visibility.

JAL 1628 is a cargo 747 transporting wine from Paris to Tokyo with a refueling break in Anchorage, Alaska. Our airplane pilot is one Mr Kenju Terauchi. He is a veteran aviator with over 10,000 hours of flight time, including experience as a fighter pilot. Other crew members include his co-pilot Takanori Tamefuji and the flight engineer Yoshio Tsukuda.

They're cruising through the skies routinely when suddenly Captain Terauchi notices lights off to the left side of the 747. Two bright lights, keeping pace with the plane. At first, he thinks they might be military aircraft. This is Alaska, after all, and there are military bases everywhere.

But these lights aren't behaving like any aircraft he knows. They are too close! They are moving with accuracy and are keeping pace with the 747 at about 600 mph at cruise.

Next, the lights move in front of the plane.

The Walnut-Shaped Craft

What Captain Terauchi sees next defies everything he knows about aviation. Remember, this is a highly experience airplane pilot with thousands of hours of flight.

It is a massive craft. He describes it as walnut-shaped, dark, with two rectangular glowing sections that look like arrays of lights or engines. It is effing ginormous! He estimates it being as big as TWO aircraft carriers! And it's hovering so close in front of his plane that he can feel its heat on his face through the cockpit window.

Yes... heat! From an object in the freezing air at 35,000 feet!

The team is totally shocked! They are observing this object, attempting to determine its identity. It can't be an airplane because they don't move this way. It isn't a helicopter because helicopters cannot operate at 35,000 feet. It obviously isn't some balloon because they can't keep up with a 747, or go faster than it for that matter!

For minutes the object remains ahead of them. Terauchi requests permission from air traffic control to change course, to see if the object will follow. He banks left and the object follows. He banks right and it still follows. It's tracking them deliberately, staying with them.

Suddenly, it moves to the side and takes up a position off their left wing, still pacing them.

The Confirmation

There are many reasons why this case is remarkable: it wasn't just the 747 crew witnessing this. Air traffic control radar in Anchorage, AL recorded the object. The FAA confirmed radar contact. The military radar at Elmendorf Air Force Base confirmed radar contact.

Several independent ground-based radar systems detected what the pilots were observing.

John Callahan, who was the Division Chief of the FAAs Accidents and Investigations Branch, at that time subsequently testified that he was assigned to examine this case. He analyzed the radar information, the cockpit audio recordings and the pilot statements. He confirmed: there was definitely something there. Something large and something that showed up on multiple, totally independent, radar systems.

The object stayed with JAL 1628 for about 50 minutes. Fifty minutes of multiple witnesses, multiple sensor confirmations, documented communication with air traffic control. And then, finally, it just... left. It shot off at an incredible speed and just disappeared.

The FAA Investigation and Cover-Up

The FAA launched an official investigation. They interviewed the crew and analyzed the radar data. They compiled a comprehensive report.

Wanna guess who decided to showed up? According to John Callahan, representatives from the CIA, FBI, and Reagan's Scientific Study Team came to the FAA headquarters for a briefing. They reviewed everything including the tapes, the data, the radar returns, and the witness statements.

And at the end of the meeting, Callahan says, they were told: "This event never happened. We were never here. You are to say nothing about this."

The investigation was classified and the data was seized. The witnesses were told to stay quiet.

However, Callahan retained duplicates and years later in 2001 he revealed the story publicly at the National Press Club sharing the proof and testimonies. So, initially there was refusal. Eventually there was acceptance.

Why JAL 1628 Matters

This wasn't a military encounter where you could claim it's classified for national security reasons. This was a commercial airline flight with a civilian crew. You have air traffic control and the FAA, a civilian agency, conducting the investigation.

And the object was confirmed by multiple independent radar systems. This wasn't a visual misidentification. This wasn't planet Venus or some stupid swamp gas. This was something solid enough to create radar returns, large enough to pace a freakin' 747, and maneuverable enough to track the aircraft through course changes for nearly an hour.

The fact that the investigation was shut down and classified tells you everything you need to know. The official story became that Captain Terauchi had "misidentified" lights from another aircraft, despite the radar confirmations and multiple witnesses.

But the evidence exists. The radar data was documented and the witnesses came forward. It showed that the phenomenon wasn't limited to military encounters. It was happening in civilian airspace, to civilian pilots, in ways that couldn't be hidden or dismissed.

Their denial is slowly crumbling.

March 13, 1997: The Phoenix Lights

Now, my beautiful people, let's discuss one of the most well-known mass UFO encounters in recent history. This case stands out because it didn't occur above a remote forest or within secured military zones. Instead it took place over an American city observed by thousands of ordinary citizens many of whom recorded it on video.

It's early evening on March 13, 1997 in Phoenix, Arizona. The skies are nice and clear.

At 7:30 PM, residents began noticing an unusual sight in the sky to the north of Phoenix. A massive cluster of lights set in a V-formation drifting quietly from the northwest toward the southeast. Not just a few people either. Initially hundreds noticed it then the count rose to thousands spanning hundreds of miles from Henderson, Nevada through Phoenix and extending down, to Tucson.

This wasn't a fleeting glimpse either. This thing was visible for hours, moving slowly and deliberately across the entire state of Arizona.

The Craft

There was a consistent description by the observers: a massive V-shaped craft which was dark and blocking out the stars as it passed overhead. Those who saw it from close up said it was absolutely enormous! Some estimates range from one to two miles wide! One or two miles!! Can you picture gazing up and witnessing something a mile or more in width floating quietly over your town?

There were lights positioned along the edge... five, six or seven lights set in a V-shape. Some witnesses described additional lights on the underside. The lights were steady, not blinking like aircraft lights. The object glided quietly and steadily at a slow pace, perhaps around 30 mph or slower.

Individuals hurried outdoors carrying their cameras.

People rushed outside with their cameras. They called local news stations and within an hour, the phone lines at Luke Air Force Base were lighting up with reports. The Arizona Daily News was flooded with calls. Local TV stations started receiving calls and videos.

This wasn't just a few random sightings. This was a statewide event witnessed by thousands. Thousands of people were reporting the sighting to the police, other authorities, and to the press.

The Videos

Multiple people captured video footage. The most well-known is the footage filmed around 10:00 PM displaying a sequence of lights aligned horizontally over Phoenix. However the key point is this: there were in fact two occurrences that evening.

The first event, happening at 7:30 PM involved the massive V-shaped object moving through the state. The subsequent event, near 10:00 PM consisted of fixed lights seen above the Phoenix region. The military later stated that these 10:00 PM lights were flares released during a training drill at the Barry Goldwater Range.

Okay, maybe those later lights were actually flares. But what about the 7:30 PM object? The massive craft that hundreds of witnesses saw, that blocked out stars, that moved steadily across 300+ miles? That wasn't flares. That wasn't a training exercise. Flares light up the sky and then can be clearly seen falling down to the ground. They don't float or travel for hundreds of miles. It is simply not possible.

The Governor's Admission

The governor of Arizona at the time was Fife Symington. A few months after the sightings, he held a press conference where he had his chief of staff dress up in an alien costume as a joke, essentially mocking the witnesses and ridiculing the entire incident.

But ten years later, in 2007, Governor Symington came clean. He admitted that he saw the object too. He was watching it from his yard. And it was "enormous and inexplicable."

In a CNN interview, he said: "I'm a pilot and I know just about every machine that flies. It was bigger than anything that I've ever seen. It remains a great mystery. Other people saw it, responsible people. I don't know why people would ridicule it."

He continued to say that his joke press conference of 1997 was because he was concerned about mass panic and wanted to maintain people's calm. However, he later regretted the mockery because what people saw was real and that he had insulted the residents who had seen it.

The sitting governor of a U.S. State confessing ten years afterward that indeed he witnessed it and no it wasn't just ordinary planes or flares.

The Documentation

Dr. Lynne Kitei, a doctor based in Phoenix, captured images of the Phoenix Lights several times (there were other sightings before and after the famous March 13 event). She dedicated years to researching, talking to observers and gathering evidence. Her records are comprehensive, consisting of hundreds of testimonies, videos and photos taken from various spots and viewpoints all depicting the same phenomenon.

The witnesses include several police officers, pilots, military personnel, doctors, lawyers, and everyday citizens. Credible, professional people who know the difference between conventional aircraft and something extraordinary.

Why the Phoenix Lights Matter

This was a mass sighting. It wasn't just one or two witnesses who could be easily dismissed. Thousands of people across an entire American state, many with video cameras, experienced it.

The military's explanation of flares doesn't hold up for the 7:30 PM event. Flares don't move in formation across 300 miles. Flares don't block out stars. Flares don't maintain steady altitude and speed for hours.

And the fact that the governor himself saw it and later admitted it was real? That's significant. It showed that the ridicule and dismissal that witnesses often face comes from fear and uncertainty, not from genuine investigation.

The Phoenix Lights forced a conversation and major news networks covered it. Documentaries were made. The sheer number of witnesses made it impossible to completely bury or dismiss this mass sighting.

It was more breakage in their official denials. Another piece of evidence that couldn't be explained away. An additional stride toward disclosure. Keep pushing, everyone! Keep breaking it down! We're making progress, bit by bloody bit!

November 14, 2004: The USS Nimitz and the "Tic Tac" Incident

Alright, now we're at the big kahuna. This is the case that changed everything. The encounter that would eventually lead to the Pentagon admitting that yes, UFOs are real, and no, they don't know what they are. The narrative has started to change...

Now, we're on the southwest of San Diego, 100 miles off the coast, on November the 14th, 2004. The USS Nimitz Carrier Strike Group is engaged in training exercises. BTW this is one of the most technologically advanced naval operations in the world. There's multiple ships, multiple aircraft, state-of-the-art radar systems, the world's top-notch infrared tracking systems... it's the works, folks. These are the big boys who have the big toys! You don't wanna mess around with these guys!

Many days before November 14, the radar systems on the USS Princeton, a guided-missile cruiser in the strike group, have been tracking unusual activity in the sky. There are objects that aren't registering as normal aircraft. They were seen at 80,000 feet, which is far higher than commercial aviation, and then dropping to sea level within seconds. Then they're disappearing and then reappearing abruptly.

The radar operators are totally baffled. Senior Chief Kevin Day, one of the operators, documents everything. These objects are behaving in ways that are impossible and yet they keep popping up daily.

On November 14 a pair of F/A-18 Super Hornets is dispatched for an investigation. The flying team includes Commander David Fravor and Lieutenant Commander Jim Slaight in one jet while a separate pilot-WSO duo operates the second plane.

What follows is among the most extensively recorded and examined UFO incidents in history.

The Encounter

Fravor and his squad are directed to the spot where the Princeton's radar detects an object. The day is clear with perfect visibility. They are flying at 20,000 feet when Fravor glances down and notices something disturbing the water surface below them.

The ocean is turbulent. It churns as if something lies beneath the surface, possibly submerged, causing the disturbance. He attempts to identify the source when his WSO Jim Slaight notices something.

There's an object hovering above the water disturbance.

Fravor later describes the object as looking like a giant Tic Tac, white and smooth, with no wings, and no exhaust. The thing is about 40 feet long, shaped like an elongated pill, or Tic Tac, whichever one you prefer. It simply lingers there 50 feet above the ocean.

Fravor makes a decision. He's going to check this thing out. He puts his aircraft into a descending spiral, moving down to get a closer look. As he descends, the object begins to mirror his movement. It starts ascending and spiraling up toward him. They're circling each other, closing distance and getting closer.

And then, suddenly, the object does something that should be impossible.

The Impossible Maneuver

As Fravor continues his descent, trying to cut off the object and get closer, the Tic Tac suddenly accelerates. No, not a steady acceleration, but instant. Fravor describes it as going from a hover to supersonic speed in less than a second. Not a sound, or a sonic boom, or any signs of visible propulsion. It just... shoots off into the distance.

And where does it go? Sixty miles away. To the Combat Air Patrol (CAP) point—the exact location where Fravor's aircraft was supposed to be patrolling, information that was only known to people with access to the strike group's flight plan.

How did it know? That is the million dollar question.

The USS Princeton's radar tracked the object making that 60-mile jump. Senior Chief Day confirms it. The object appeared at their CAP point almost instantaneously from its previous position.

Fravor and his squad return to the Nimitz to report their observations. The commander promptly sends out another plane to check it out. It's flown by Commander Chad Underwood. This flight carries a targeting device, the ATFLIR system, which is essentially an infrared camera made to detect and capture heat signatures.

The FLIR Video

Underwood finds the object. He locks onto it with the ATFLIR system and he records it. That video which is officially called "FLIR1" or the "Tic Tac video" is now one of the most famous pieces of UFO evidence in existence.

In the video, you can hear Underwood and his WSO reacting in real-time. The object is moving erratically and they're trying to track it. At the end of the video, it accelerates off-screen so fast that the tracking system can't keep up with it.

You can hear them say: "Whoa! Got it! ... Whoa!"

The footage stayed confidential for 13 years until it was publicly released in 2017. Later in 2019, the U.S. Navy officially acknowledged the video's legitimacy and confessed they didn't know what the object was. However this acknowledgment is what holds all the significance.

The Performance Data

Lets discuss the actions of this object according to the radar information pilot reports and sensor data.

Altitude changes: The object fell from 28,000 feet down to sea level within 0.78 seconds. That's a descent rate that would generate forces that would destroy any known aircraft and kill any human pilot instantly. We're referring to G-forces over 5,000 Gs. Humans lose consciousness at 9 Gs and pass out. Were there any beings on-board this craft or is it some type of drone?

Acceleration: The object accelerated from a hover to supersonic speeds instantaneously. No aircraft can do that. Acceleration requires thrust, which requires fuel, which creates heat and exhaust. This thing had none of that and achieved a lot more than a fuel engine.

No visible means of propulsion: No wings, no tail, no exhaust, no contrails, no heat signature from engines. It defied the basic principles of aerodynamics and propulsion which we have today.

Trans-medium capability: The object appeared to move seamlessly from air to water and back, based on the water disturbance and the radar tracking. That's not something our aircraft can do.

Knew their flight plan: It went to the exact CAP point. That information wasn't public. That suggests awareness, intelligence, advanced sensor capabilities. How much do these things know?

The Witnesses Go Public

For years, this incident was classified. The pilots and crew couldn't talk about it. However, in 2017, Commander Fravor started speaking and sharing his account publicly. He has given interviews to major media outlets like 60 Minutes, CNN, The New York Times. He's appeared on Joe Rogan's podcast and explained the encounter in mad detail. He has testified before Congress.

And his story never changes. He's consistent, credible, and

unshakable. He knows what he saw. He knows it wasn't conventional technology and he's putting his reputation on the line to tell the truth. These people are the heroes of the UFO study. The ones who risk it all for the truth.

Lieutenant Ryan Graves, another Navy pilot who had multiple encounters with UAPs during training exercises off the East Coast (we'll get to that later), has also testified to Congress alongside Fravor. Testifying to the American Congress is a very big step for legitimacy.

These aren't random civilians making insane claims. These are top-tier military aviators with impeccable credentials, saying on the record: we encountered technology that shouldn't exist.

Why Nimitz Changed Everything

The Nimitz incident is the watershed moment. Here's why:

- **Multiple sensor confirmations:** Radar, infrared, visual sighting and various independent systems each detected the object.
- **Multiple highly credible witnesses:** Navy pilots, weapons systems officers, radar operators. These are all highly trained professionals.
- **Official Pentagon confirmation:** In 2017, the Pentagon acknowledged the FLIR1 video was real. In 2019, the Navy confirmed it was authentic footage of an unidentified aerial phenomenon, a UAP. That is legit significant.
- **Performance that defies known physics:** The object's capabilities like the acceleration, the speed, the lack of propulsion, can't be explained by any known human technology.
- **Chain of custody for evidence:** The video came from

official Navy sources. The radar data was documented. This isn't some grainy amateur footage, this is military-grade sensor data. This is the world's most capable equipment.

The Nimitz encounter became public knowledge in 2017 thanks to investigative journalism by The New York Times and the efforts of former Pentagon official Luis Elizondo (we'll talk more about him in the next chapter). And once it was out, the Pentagon couldn't put the genie back in the bottle.

They had to admit it. They were compelled to acknowledge that yes, this happened. No, we don't know what it was, and yes, it concerns us.

The Nimitz Tic Tac incident broke their denial and it forced disclosure to begin. Yippee!

2014-2015: The USS Roosevelt Encounters

But Nimitz wasn't a one-off case. It wasn't an isolated incident that could be dismissed as an anomaly. Because from 2014 to 2015, pilots operating off the aircraft carrier USS Roosevelt, stationed off the East Coast of the United States, were encountering these objects regularly.

It wasn't just once or twice either… it was multiple times per week for months.

Lieutenant Ryan Graves, an F/A-18 Super Hornet pilot with ten years of experience, has spoken extensively about these encounters. During training missions near the Virginia coastline, he and his squadron repeatedly encountered these objects.

The Frequency

The incidents were not rare. Graves has said that after they upgraded their radar systems in 2014, they started detecting these objects constantly. They'd be out on training missions, and there they were. Objects moving in ways that shouldn't be possible, showing up on radar and infrared systems very frequently.

Sometimes the objects would hold position in high winds. They'd be hovering at 30,000 feet in 120-mph winds without moving. That's not aerodynamically possible for conventional aircraft. You'd need constant thrust to maintain position, which means heat, which means infrared signature. These objects had no heat signature.

Sometimes they'd track the jets, following them through maneuvers.

And sometimes, they came dangerously close. Graves reported multiple near-misses. These weren't distant objects, these were objects came dangerously close within 100 feet of his aircraft. That's really terrifying and threatening when you're moving at hundreds of miles per hour.

The "Gimbal" and "Go Fast" Videos

Two more videos from these East Coast encounters were officially released by the Pentagon in 2017, alongside the Nimitz Tic Tac video.

The first video, called "Gimbal," shows an object rotating in mid-flight. The pilots' reactions can be heard: "Look at that thing, dude!" "It's rotating!" The object appears to be a disc or sphere, glowing, moving against the wind, and then it rotates completely, something conventional aircraft don't do.

The second video, "Go Fast," shows an object skimming low over the ocean at high speed. The infrared camera tracks it as it moves rapidly across the water. The pilots are trying to lock onto it, and you can hear their excitement: "Whoa! Got it!"

Both videos show objects moving in ways that defy conventional aerodynamics. Both were captured on advanced military infrared targeting systems and both were confirmed authentic by the Navy.

The Safety Concern

So what pushed Graves to speak publicly? It was safety. He and his fellow pilots filed official hazard reports because these objects were creating dangerous conditions that could mean life or death.

But when they reported these incidents up the usual chain of command, they hit a wall. Nobody wanted to discuss it and absolutely nobody wanted to investigate. The official attitude seemed to be: file your report, but don't make a big deal about it, got it?

That was unacceptable to Graves. These are active military training areas and if there are unknown objects operating in these areas, the military needs to address it. They need to either identify what they are or take steps to avoid them. These objects were clearly a threat.

Congressional Testimony

In July 2023, Lieutenant Ryan Graves testified before Congress alongside Commander David Fravor and intelligence official David Grusch (we'll talk about Grusch in the next chapter). He described the encounters in detail, explained the safety concerns, and called for transparent investigation and reporting protocols.

His testimony was powerful because he wasn't claiming aliens. He wasn't speculating about origin. He was simply stating facts: we encountered objects that we couldn't identify, they operated in restricted airspace, they demonstrated advanced capabilities, and they pose a potential safety risk.

That's not conspiracy theory. That's documented military reality. It's available for you to see online yourself.

Why the Roosevelt Encounters Matter

Nimitz in 2004 could maybe be dismissed as a one-time event. Strange, yes. Unexplained, yup. But maybe an anomaly.

The Roosevelt encounters from 2014-2015 showed that no, this is ongoing. It's frequent. It's happening in multiple locations and it's concerning enough that trained military pilots are filing safety reports and speaking publicly about it.

The detection of these objects following radar upgrades implies they may have been present all along but went unnoticed with our previous technology. With our new capabilities we're now coming to understand the extent of the phenomenon.

These encounters directly led to the Navy establishing official reporting protocols for UAPs. In 2019, the Navy issued new guidelines for pilots to report unexplained aerial phenomena without fear of ridicule or career damage. That's a huge shift—acknowledging that this is real enough to need official reporting procedures.

Their denial wasn't just cracking anymore. Pieces were actually falling off. It's happening, boys & girls!

April 25, 2013: Aguadilla, Puerto Rico

Let me show you one more case, because this one demonstrates something we haven't talked about yet: trans-medium capability. The ability for these objects to move seamlessly from one medium, air, to another medium, water.

April 25, 2013. Aguadilla, Puerto Rico. A U.S. Customs and Border Protection (CBP) aircraft, a DHC-8 turboprop equipped with an advanced infrared camera system is on patrol near Rafael Hernández Airport.

At 9:20 PM the team spots an object on infrared. It's gliding close to the water at 20-30 feet above the surface and moving at an extremely fast pace There are no visible lights and no transponder. There is no radio communication. It's simply a heat signature moving erratically.

The Footage

The CBP plane follows and records the object for about three minutes. The infrared footage is just stunning because it's high-quality and stabilized. The video shows the UAP performing maneuvers that are... well, frankly, *impossible* for us to do at this time.

The object travels at velocities measured between 40 and 120 mph. It shifts direction swiftly with turns that demand extreme G-forces. Then it enters the water. You can see it on the infrared footage doing that. The object lowers, itself touches the water surface, and dives beneath. There is no splash or ripple on the water's surface whatsoever. It simply slips in. Slips out. Sheesh! That's really impressive!

The object continues moving underwater. They can track the heat signature underwater for a time. Then in a stranger turn, the object seems to divide into two individual objects underwater. Two separate heat signatures, each moving on its own. Doesn't that blow your mind!?

Finally, one of the UAPs re-surfaces from the water and continues flying through the air. Again, there is no splash or disruption on the water's surface. It has a total seamless transition from water to air as if there was no barrier at all.

The Scientific Analysis

This video was leaked in 2013. Subsequently, the footage went through an extensive scientific examination by the Scientific Coalition for UAP Studies (SCU), an organization of scientists, engineers and military experts who investigate UFO data and evidence.

Their 2015 report is comprehensive. They reviewed the video's chain of custody and verified it originated from a CBP airplane. Measured the objects velocity and path and studied the infrared signature. Their finding: that the object showed features not matching with any known aircraft, drone or natural phenomenon.

The trans-medium capability, moving from air to water without slowing down, without creating disturbance, is something we don't have technology to do. Submarines are very slow. Aircraft can't operate underwater. Drones can't seamlessly transition between mediums. We simply cannot do what this thing was doing. It simply cannot be done.

Whatever this was, it operated in ways that defy our engineering capabilities.

Why Aguadilla Matters

This case matters because:

1. **It's recent.** It took place in 2013, not many years ago. This is modern, contemporary evidence.
2. **High-quality footage.** This isn't grainy, ambiguous video. This is professional-grade infrared from a government aircraft.
3. **Trans-medium capability.** This demonstrates that these objects aren't just aerial, they can operate in multiple environments seamlessly.
4. **Scientific analysis.** The SCU report applied rigorous scientific methodology to analyze the footage. This wasn't amateur speculation, this was proper scientific investigation.
5. **Official source.** The footage came from a U.S. government aircraft engaged in official patrol operations. The chain of custody is properly documented.

The Aguadilla incident demonstrates that the phenomenon continues and is not confined to military drills and that these objects possess abilities going way beyond mere flight maneuvers.

It's more evidence. More breaks in their denial, everyone! More pressure building towards disclosure.

How These Cases Bring Disclosure Closer

Alright, lets pause a sec and review what we have learned in this chapter.

Rendlesham Forest (1980): Numerous military personnel testified, there was physical proof, and an official document/memo existed. The UK government later made the records public verifying the probe did in fact take place and that it was regarded very seriously. It demonstrated that this phenomenon was not limited to the U.S. but that NATO partners experienced it as well and that such objects could appear at our most secure nuclear sites with impunity.

Japan Airlines 1628 (1986): Commercial aviation, FAA investigation, several radar pings. The FAA took it seriously enough to investigate thoroughly before the investigation was shut down and classified. It showed the phenomenon wasn't just military. It was happening in civilian airspace as well.

Phoenix Lights (1997): Thousands of witnesses, among them the state governor who eventually admitted he observed it too. Multiple videos. Media coverage. It showed that mass sightings couldn't be dismissed or hidden. The sheer number of witnesses made ridicule insufficient as a cover-up strategy. That strategy just couldn't work here.

USS Nimitz (2004): Pentagon-confirmed video, multiple sensor systems, highly credible military witnesses. Commander Fravor's testimony given in public put a face and a voice directly on the ongoing phenomenon. When the Pentagon published the footage in 2017 and verified its authenticity in 2019, it was a landmark event. Official recognition was received. Hooray!

USS Roosevelt (2014-2015): Ongoing incidents, security issues, official Navy documentation procedures and reporting protocols put in place. Lieutenant Graves' 2023 congressional testimony presented the matter to legislators. It showed that this is current, it's frequent, and it's something the military can no longer ignore. It has been exposed.

Aguadilla (2013): Trans-medium capability, scientific analysis, high-quality documentation. It demonstrated that the phenomenon has capabilities beyond what we've imagined, and that scientific investigation is not only possible but necessary. We cannot sit on this any longer.

Do you see the progression? Each case added pressure. Each case made denial harder to maintain. Each case brought more evidence, more witnesses, more documentation.

With every case, an increasing number of people began asking: why do we keep rejecting this? Why do we continue acting like this is fake?

The Shift in Public Discourse

Something fundamental changed between 1947 and now. Back in the day, in 1947, the response to UFO reports was denial, ridicule, and dismissal. Project Grudge was literally designed to debunk and explain away sightings as if they were jokes.

However, by the 2010s that tactic no longer proved effective. The evidence was too good and too frequent. The witnesses were too credible and our technology had advanced to the point where you couldn't just say "weather balloon" and expect the public to believe it.

The Pentagon's release of the Nimitz, Gimbal and Go Fast clips in 2017 marked a significant milestone. It was the first time in modern history that the U.S. Military formally confirmed that UFOs do exist, and that we possess recordings, and that their nature remains unidentified. Two thumbs up here!

That admission opened the floodgates. Pilots started coming forward. Former military and intelligence officials started speaking publicly and our Congress started holding hearings. Despite being limited, the government *did* start listening.

Their narrative shifted from "UFOs do not exist" to "UFOs do exist. What exactly are they?"

This marks the start of disclosure; it is not the disclosure itself. We're not there yet. But the beginning of it includes the acknowledgment that the phenomenon is real and worthy of serious investigation.

The Path Forward

So what position does that put us in?

We find ourselves at a crucial point. Official recognition is underway, though complete openness and transparency has not been reached yet. We remain uncertain about what these objects are, what their origin is, or what their intent is. We don't know the extent of the government's knowledge now or in the past. We do not know which evidence remains classified, still stored away in some hidden vault.

However, we are closer than we have ever been. That is a great sign.

The next chapter will be about exploring the current disclosure process in greater detail. We will discuss the whistleblowers who have come forward, the hearings at Congress that have occurred, the official statements from the Pentagon, and the newly established government offices responsible for investigating UAPs.

We will examine what disclosure may actually entail. I'm not referring to the Hollywood portrayal. I mean the messy, complex reality of a government gradually acknowledging decades of hidden secrets.

We will ask the big questions: What happens once disclosure is complete? In what ways does society transform when we formally admit that we are not alone? What implications does this have for science, religion, philosophy, politics and our perception of humanity's role in the universe?

That's the direction we're moving in, my Great friend! Regardless of whether it happens in one year or a decade, disclosure is inevitable. The evidence is overwhelmingly convincing. The testimonies are highly credible. The demand from the public is intense. Everyone wants more transparency. We must be part of it.

The truth cannot stay hidden forever.

Let's find out what happens.

CHAPTER 7

DISCLOSURE: THE MOMENT IS HERE

Alright, you Gorgeous people, remember our discussion about the recurring pattern of denial? How from 1947 onwards the government has dealt with UFOs by privately conducting investigations but publicly rejecting their existence? How witnesses who came forward have been mocked, evidence was kept under wraps, and the official narrative consistently telling the public "there's nothing to see here, keep it moving"?

Well... that pattern is shifting... it's changing quite a bit, homes!

I mean, it's actually shifting in real-time, like right now. We are living through it.

Denial has been blocking us, for what, over 70 years? It is being broken down. Slowly and chaotically, but hot diggity, it is being broken down!

I have to say it is very thrilling to be alive in these times.

The events unfolding now are unlike anything seen before. The U.S. Government, yes the same government that has dismissed these matters for years, is now finally acknowledging them. The Pentagon is releasing footage, while Congress is conducting hearings. Pilots are giving sworn testimony and whistleblowers are stepping up with explosive allegations and evidence.

Disclosure isn't a future occurrence, people! It is taking place now!

Let me guide you through the journey that brought us here. Let's discuss the events of past years and their significance, because we are at that moment in the story where everything shifts gears and changes what lies ahead.

December 16, 2017: The Day Things Fell Apart

Imagine this: It's a Saturday morning. Most of America is preparing for the holidays finishing up last-minute Christmas shopping... or perhaps still in bed asleep. The New York Times decides to drop a bombshell.

NY Times Headline: "Glowing Auras and 'Black Money': The Pentagon's Mysterious U.F.O. Program"

Authored by Helene Cooper, Ralph Blumenthal and Leslie Kean the article reveals what most people don't know: the Pentagon had been conducting a covert UFO research initiative named the Advanced Aerospace Threat Identification Program, or AATIP.

Wait, what? Say that again.

The U.S. Department of Defense/Pentagon? The very agency that has been insisting for years that UFOs don't exist and that anyone believing in them is crazy? *They've actually been covertly researching UFOs all this while?* Get the fudge outta here!

Yup. Those very same people. Now, I don't know about you, but in my humble opinion I think that someone would only investigate things they believed were real, right? Do you know anyone looking into the existence of unicorns or werewolves? The first thing would be you believe they exist in order to go forward into investigating them.

The Program Nobody Knew About

AATIP was established in 2007, tucked away in the "black budget"—the classified funding that Congress allocates for secret programs. It was run out of the Defense Intelligence Agency, and its mission was to investigate reports of unidentified aerial phenomena, particularly those encountered by military personnel.

The initiative was primarily launched thanks to the work of Senator Harry Reid from Nevada, who secured $22 million bucks in funding. The inquiries were carried out by a contractor named Bigelow Aerospace owned by billionaire Robert Bigelow (who has openly declared that he is "absolutely convinced" that extraterrestrials exist and have visited Earth).

AATIP gathered reports, examined data, commissioned research on propulsion technology and looked into events such as the Nimitz incident mentioned in the previous chapter. They took this seriously. This was not basic research, this was the Pentagon backed by financial support and assets examining the UFO phenomena.

Then in 2012 the finances ran out. At least that's the official story. The program officially ended, though some former officials have said the work continued informally.

Enter Luis Elizondo

So who brought all this to light? Meet Luis Elizondo.

Elizondo served at the Pentagon for than two decades, including a period at the Office of the Under Secretary of Defense for Intelligence. He held the position of director of AATIP from 2010 to 2017. According to him, his frustration was growing steadily.

Why? Because the program continuously uncovered evidence of extraordinary craft, performing insane maneuvers which are deemed impossible, objects that lack apparent propulsion, and encounters that defied explanation. Yet, there was no support from leadership including no funding and certainly no willingness to take it seriously at higher levels. Even worse, there was an active stigma and ridicule around the topic. Sounds about right...

In October 2017, Elizondo resigned from the Pentagon in protest. He wrote a resignation letter addressed to Secretary of Defense James Mattis, which stated:

"Why aren't we spending more time and effort on this issue?... Despite overwhelming evidence at both the classified and unclassified levels, certain individuals in the Department

remain staunchly opposed to further research on what could be a tactical threat to our pilots, sailors, and soldiers, and perhaps even an existential threat to our national security."

He highlighted the highest levels of secrecy, the insufficient resources, and the "serious national security implications" of disregarding or ignoring this issue.

And then he went public. That was a very smart move, in my personal opinion.

Elizondo joined forces with "To The Stars Academy of Arts & Science," an organization established by Tom DeLonge (yup, it's the punk rock musician guy from Blink-182 and yes that itself is an intriguing story). The declared goal of To The Stars Academy was to promote the study of phenomena and share trustworthy/credible info to the public.

And that is exactly what they did. Bravo!

The Three Videos

In addition to the New York Times article, 3 videos were published. These were not home-videos recorded on a personal cellphone. Instead these were official military infrared recordings taken by Navy pilots during training drills.

You already know these videos from the last chapter:

- **"FLIR1" (the "Tic Tac" video)** from the USS Nimitz encounter in 2004
- **"Gimbal"** from the USS Roosevelt encounters off the East Coast in 2015
- **"Go Fast"** also from the Roosevelt encounters

These clips showed UAPs performing movements that contradicted physics. Moreover, the Pentagon was unable to refute them as they were Department of Defense recordings.

The publics response was... varied, to say the least. Certain individuals were enthusiastic, while others doubtful and some outright wrote it off as a diversion or conspiracy theory. However, the crucial point was that it sparked a dialogue. Prominent news organizations reported on it prompting questions. More people, then more, then more... you get the idea.

And the Pentagon? Well, they tried to downplay it at first, but they couldn't put the genie back in the bottle, unfortunately.

2019: The Navy's Confirmation

Jump to September 2019. The U.S. Navy officially acknowledges what was already clear to all who saw the footage: the recordings are authentic. The items shown in the videos remain unidentified.

Allow me to restate that to make it clear: <u>The American Navy has formally acknowledged the existence of UFOs</u>.

Admittedly, they avoided the term "UFOs." Instead they said "UAPs" (Unidentified Aerial Phenomena) since re-branding and changing the name makes it seem less frightening or whatever... Putting terminology aside, this was a major event.

Navy spokesperson Joseph Gradisher stated in a message to The Black Vault (a website that preserves government records):

"The Navy designates the objects contained in these videos as unidentified aerial phenomena."

He additionally acknowledged that the videos should *never*

have been made public. Oops! Sorry, not sorry! Given that they were already available, the Navy was not going to dispute their legitimacy.

What is more important is that approximately at the same time, the Navy introduced new instructions and guidelines for pilots to document UAP encounters. They developed protocols, paperwork and systems, as pilots were frequently coming across these phenomena and the Navy ultimately recognized this as a serious matter requiring appropriate reporting methods. They also need this for better control themselves.

Think about what that means. For all those decades, the pilots who reported UFO… I mean UAP sightings were laughed at, dismissed, sometimes even grounded. Now, the Navy was saying: "Yeah, this is real. Please report it. We need to track this."

That's a complete 180 degrees. What a shift! That's why this is all so exciting.

2020-2021: Task Forces and Official Reports

In August 2020 the Pentagon formally set up the Unidentified Aerial Phenomena Task Force (UAPTF). Its purpose: to detect, examine and document UAPs that might represent a risk to U.S. national security.

Consider that once again. The Pentagon established an official task force to examine UFOs. It was not done covertly, but openly. They have made it public.

Then in June 2021 the Office of the Director of National Intelligence (ODNI) published a document that captured attention worldwide: the "Preliminary Assessment: Unidentified Aerial Phenomena."

This report to Congress, was required by Congress itself, under the 2021 Intelligence Authorization Act. Congress sought answers. They insisted on a detailed account of the governments knowledge regarding UAPs.

What the Report Said

The analysis covered 144 incidents documented by U.S. Government agencies from November 2004 to March 2021. The majority of these were accounts from pilots, alongside information collected from sensors and radar technology.

Out of those 144 cases, the report managed to clarify *ONLY ONE* with strong certainty. One out of one hundred and forty-four. It turned out to be a big deflating balloon.

The remaining 143 are still without explanation. Wowza!

Allow me to share with you important excerpts from this official government document:

"UAP clearly pose a safety of flight issue and may pose a challenge to U.S. national security."

"Most of the UAP reported probably do represent physical objects given that a majority of UAP were registered across multiple sensors, to include radar, infrared, electro-optical, weapon seekers, and visual observation."

And to spice things up more...:

"Some UAP appeared to remain stationary in winds aloft, move against the wind, maneuver abruptly, or move at considerable speed, without discernible means of propulsion. In a small number of cases, military aircraft systems processed radio frequency (RF) energy associated with UAP sightings."

Thus the U.S. Government in an official report presented to Congress acknowledged that:

- These objects are real (multiple sensors confirm)
- They pose a safety and security issue
- They perform maneuvers that shouldn't be possible
- They have no visible means of propulsion
- Some of them emit radio frequency energy

That's basically the Pentagon saying: "Yeah, bro. Something real is out there. We don't know WTF it is. We are concerned."

That's disclosure, my friend. Not full disclosure, far from it. It's a start and a promising one, at that.

May 2022: Congress Holding Public Hearings

Okay, so now we get to something that hadn't happened in over 50 years: a public congressional hearing on UFOs.

On May 17 2022, the House Intelligence Subcommittee on Counterterrorism, Counterintelligence, and Counterproliferation, conducted a public session named "Unidentified Aerial Phenomena: Exposing the Truth."

Seriously? The United States Congress, the lawmaking arm of our government, conducted a public hearing on UFOs? The previous instance was in 1969 just before Project Blue Book was shut down. This is significant news, people!

Who Testified

Two Pentagon officials testified:

1. **Scott Bray**, Deputy Director of Naval Intelligence
2. **Ronald Moultrie**, Under Secretary of Defense for Intelligence and Security

These were very senior intelligence officials, not low-level employees, who testified under oath in front of Congress on national television.

Bray presented the committee with UAP footage, one of which depicted a spherical object swiftly passing by a military plane. He verified that reported UAP encounters had risen to more than 400 since the initial evaluation was released.

Four hundred mother-loving incidents. And that's just what's been officially reported. The ones which are off the books must be beyond extraordinary!

He also admitted that certain objects display "flight characteristics or performance capabilities that we can't explain with the data we have available"

The hearing was largely professional, concentrating on the national security ramifications, the necessity for data gathering and reducing stigma so that pilots can feel at ease reporting. But it was also historic. Because it was Congress, publicly, taking this seriously. FINALLY! YESSSS!!

There were no jokes or dismissals. It was just: "This is very serious and we must comprehend it. Let's work out what's happening."

July 2023: The Grusch Testimony

And then... oh man! Then we arrive at July 26 of 2023.

The House Oversight Committee convened a hearing, entitled "Unidentified Anomalous Phenomena: Implications on National Security, Public Safety, and Government Transparency."

Three witnesses testified:

1. **Commander David Fravor** (you know him—the Nimitz Tic Tac pilot)
2. **Lieutenant Ryan Graves** (USS Roosevelt encounters, safety advocate)
3. **David Grusch** (former intelligence official and whistleblower)

Fravor and Graves testified about their encounters, which we've already covered. But Grusch? Grusch dropped bombs on yo' momz!

Who Is David Grusch?

David Grusch is a former intelligence officer with serious credentials. He worked at the National Geospatial-Intelligence Agency (NGA) and the National Reconnaissance Office (NRO). He acted as the representative for the Unidentified Aerial Phenomena Task Force and jointly directed UAP analysis at the National Geospatial-Intelligence Agency.

Put simply this isn't any random dude. This person had access to secret information at the highest levels within the intelligence community.

In 2023 Grusch revealed himself as a whistleblower by submitting official complaints to the Intelligence Community Inspector General and sharing classified data with Congress. Subsequently in July 2023 he gave a public testimony.

What Grusch Claimed

Okay, brethren, let's slow it down, because here's what Grusch said under oath:

1. **The U.S. government has recovered non-human craft.**

He stated that the U.S. government has been recovering fragments and intact vehicles of non-human origin for decades. He said he learned this through interviews with over 40 witnesses over four years.

2. "Non-human biologics" have been recovered.

When asked directly if biologics, meaning bodies, have been recovered, Grusch answered: *"As I've stated publicly already in my News Nation interview, biologics came with some of these recoveries. Yeah."*

And when pressed on whether these were human or non-human biologics, he said: *"Non-human, and that was the assessment of people with direct knowledge on the program I talked to."*

3. There are secret crash retrieval programs.

He claimed that there are Special Access Programs operating outside of Congressional oversight that are tasked with retrieving and reverse-engineering non-human craft. He said these programs have been hidden from Congress and that funding has been misappropriated.

4. He has faced retaliation.

Grusch stated that he experienced "brutal" and "unfortunate" backlash for speaking out, though he refrained from elaborating the exact incidents during the public hearing. I believe it. Why wouldn't he? He has exposed so much... they're bound to go after him. Sorry, bruh! You know we appreciate you!

The Response

The room fell quiet at moments throughout his testimony.

Consider this: an intelligence official, sworn under oath, addressing Congress asserting that the U.S. Government holds alien spacecraft and alien bodies.

Certain members of Congress resisted, requesting proof and further information. Grusch consistently stated that he was unable to offer specifics in a forum but was prepared to share classified data with Congress in a secure setting (a SCIF).

Various Congressional members, from both the Democratic sides, appeared sincerely worried and dedicated to pursuing additional investigation.

Was Grusch telling the truth? I don't know. He's credible. He has the qualifications. He submitted whistleblower complaints indicating his claims passed through proper procedures and channels and were considered worhty of safeguarding. However, his claimed evidence has not been seen publicly.

But the fact that this testimony happened at all? That's huge! That's a former intelligence official telling Congress that we have alien spacecraft, on the record and under oath.

Whether you believe him or not, that's a pivotal moment. But think about it, if the government has openly accepted and admitted that there UFOs in the sky, why can't we believe they're in possession of one or more?

2022-Present: AARO and the Current State

In July 2022, the Pentagon created the All-domain Anomaly Resolution Office (AARO), an updated agency that succeeded the UAP Task Force and has a wider scope and mandate.

AARO's objective is to examine UAPs in every domain: air, sea, space and also the "trans-medium" class (entities traveling between these domains, such as the Aguadilla incident we mentioned before).

Dr. Sean Kirkpatrick, a physicist experienced in intelligence and scientific studies heads the office. His responsibilities include gathering reports, examining data and delivering briefings to Congress and the public.

AARO has been releasing periodic reports. By 2023 and early 2024 they obtained hundreds more reports. The majority were identified as drones, balloons, birds or other ordinary items. However a small fraction still remains genuinely unexplained despite thorough examination and analysis.

The key difference now is transparency. AARO has a public website and they release unclassified reports. They brief Congress regularly. It's not full transparency, we're still miles away, but there's still a lot of classified information and it's coming more into openness than we've had in 70 years.

Where We Are Now

This is our status as of late 2024/early 2025:

☑ **The Pentagon admits UAPs exist.** Official policy. On the record.

☑ **Congress is investigating.** Multiple hearings. Bipartisan interest. Demands for transparency.

☑ **Pilots can report without stigma.** Official reporting protocols exist. The Navy encourages reporting.

☑ **Whistleblowers are now protected and safeguarded.** Channels have been established and procedures exist for those possessing information to step forward.

☑ **The scientific community is getting involved.** Groups such as the Scientific Coalition for UAP Studies (SCU) are examining data. NASA organized a session on UAPs in 2023 and is carrying out investigations.

☑ **The media covers it seriously.** Prominent sources such as The New York Times, The Washington Post, 60 Minutes, CNN are reporting on this earnestly without ridicule.

But also:

✗ **Complete transparency is still lacking.** A significant amount of information continues to be confidential. Hopefully this can be resolved.

✗ **The nature of these objects remains unknown.** The government acknowledges their lack of knowledge (or they are keeping it from us).

✗ **Grusch's claims haven't been verified publicly.** We haven't seen the alleged recovered craft or biologics.

✗ **There's still resistance.** Some in government and media still dismiss this as nonsense.

Disclosure is underway. It's chaotic, gradual and highly complex. It's not like in movies where the President delivers a speech and reveals an alien on television

But it's real. It's happening. And we're living through it.

So What Does Disclosure Actually Mean?

Alright lets be honest for a moment and discuss the significance of all this. Not merely the politics, the hearings, and the reports... what it signifies for us. For you and me. For humanity.

Because if the government is gradually acknowledging that UFOs exist, that military members have come across them for years, that they perform movements beyond our understanding, and that if Gruschs claims are validated, that we may have even retrieved alien vehicles and remains... That changes everything!

So, my friend, lets discuss this topic. Lets consider what disclosure means for our lives and for the world around us.

For Science

If the disclosure continues and we ultimately receive confirmation that these objects aren't created by humans, whether they are extraterrestrial, or from alternate dimensions, or something completely different, then science will need to play a serious game of "catch up."

All of this is exciting! That's not a failure of science, that is science doing what it is supposed to do. When you encounter something that doesn't fit your models, you update the models. You learn and you grow.

Imagine if we could understand how these craft move. If we could imitate even a small portion of their capabilities we're talkin' groundbreaking technology, everyone! I mean there's clean energy, cutting-edge transportation, possibly even space exploration that surpasses what we presently consider achievable.

The scientific consequences are immense and I have barely even scratched the surface. Should these objects actually exist (and the proof seriously indicates they do) researchers face a new frontier to explore.

For Religion

Now this is tricky, but let's go there. Please do not get offended.

Back in Chapter 3 we talked about religious texts. We talked about how beings from the sky have been described throughout history?

What if revealing the truth proves that we are not alone? That there are other intelligent beings in the universe?

Does that conflict with religion? No. I don't think so.

The majority of scriptures do not claim that humans are the sole intelligent creatures created by God. In fact numerous texts specifically mention entities such, as angels, Jinn, devas and inhabitants of different realms. Therefore if the existence of extraterrestrial life is proven, it could actually correspond with the messages our holy writings have told us from the beginning.

Perhaps we need to revise our perspective. Rather than viewing ourselves as the center of creation, we should acknowledge that we belong to something far greater. And honestly? I find that beautiful. It doesn't make us less special, in fact it enhances the marvel of God's creation.

Various religions will respond differently, of course. There will be debates, discussions, reinterpretations and fresh theological ideas will emerge. Yet humanity has previously adjusted to paradigm shifts, such as the Earth is not the center of the universe, evolution is real, the universe is unimaginably immense, and religion has persisted and evolved.

This will be another change. Certainly a significant one. Ultimately, we'll figure it out.

For Society

Okay, this is where the ish gets complicated.

If full disclosure happens, if the government admits that yes, we've recovered craft, yes, we've been studying them, yes, we've known about this for decades, then there are going to be serious social and political consequences.

Trust in government: It was fragile to begin with, right? Now picture discovering that they have been deceiving us regarding one of the most significant findings in human history for over 70 years! The public will be furious! The public will call for responsibility and accountability. Frankly, they have every right to. The public deserves it.

Power structures: Should groundbreaking technology be revealed, particularly innovations that could transform energy, transportation or other vital sectors, it could lead to economic and political disruption. Who controls that technology? How is it distributed? Do we share it globally or hoard it nationally? These questions might spark conflict or collaboration, depending upon our approach.

Unity vs. division: One hopeful possibility is that discovering extraterrestrial life brings humanity together. We come to understand that we share this existence and that our differences are negligible. Our distinctions are tiny compared to the enormity of the universe and that our cooperation is essential to our survival. That would be truly wonderful.

However there is also a troubling possibility in which countries race to decipher and militarize extraterrestrial technology, where fear fuels discord, and where those in power take advantage for their personal gain.

The path we choose depends on us.

Handling fear: Honestly, some individuals will feel scared and that's natural. The concept of advanced beings visiting Earth, entities who are beyond our comprehension and control, is naturally unsettling and frightening. The way we address and manage that fear, how we educate the public, how we shape the narrative... all of that will be essential.

Are these visitors a threat? We don't know. At least the public doesn't. The evidence suggests they're not hostile because they've seemingly been here for decades (or longer) and haven't attacked us. But honestly, we don't know their intentions. This uncertainty generates fear. Or perhaps, they have been attacking us, but not physically, in other manners(?)

Throughout this process, education, transparency and logical discussion will be crucial.

For You, Personally

What implications does this have for you? For your life?

To begin with: it alters your perspective on the universe. You are no longer existing on a planet where humans are the sole intelligent beings. You are part of a much bigger picture. You inhabit a universe teeming with potential, with mysteries and marvels that we have yet to comprehend.

That's very humbling. It's really breathtaking.

Secondly: it pushes you to broaden your perspective and start thinking bigger. If other beings are possibly thousands or even millions of years more advanced than humans, what implications does that have for our own potential? What would humanity evolve into if we endure enough and continue gaining knowledge and keep on developing?

This serves as a reminder that we're still young. In the grand scheme of the universe, we are essentially newborn babies and possess vast potential to develop.

Third: it makes you part of this moment in history. You're living in a time when humanity's gradually yet chaotically coming to terms with the fact that we are not alone. Your grandchildren will ask about this in the future. Hey, gramps: "What was it like when disclosure happened?" And you'll be able to respond: "I was there, kiddo. I saw it unfold."

That's pretty effing cool.

The Challenges Ahead

However, lets be honest, disclosure will be complicated. We'll face difficulties that we must manage.

Secrecy and trust: Years of deception have damaged trust in the government. Restoring that faith will require time and extreme transparency. Additionally, some individuals will never regain trust in the government, no matter what. Can you really blame them?

Misinformation: In the digital era, false data and fake news travels quicker than truth. As disclosure continues, an influx of hoaxes and conspiracies and unfounded guesses will emerge. Separating signal from noise is going to be difficult.

Exploitation: Anytime there's uncertainty and fear, bad actors will exploit it. Scammers, cult leaders, political opportunists. They'll use disclosure for their own purposes and we need to be vigilant.

Technological risk: Should we obtain advanced technology, there are inherent risks. Technology itself is impartial or neutral, meaning it is capable of being used for good or bad purposes. How we handle it responsibly is a challenge we must address. That depends upon our leadership.

Psychological impact: Not everyone is going to handle this well. The beliefs of some people will be completely disrupted. Mental health support, good education, and supportive community involvement will be crucial.

These are not reasons to avoid disclosure. They are reasons to approach it with great care, with mindfulness and with compassion.

We're Living Through History

Listen, my Amazing friend, I realize this is quite intense. I understand it's a great deal to absorb. However, I trust you're experiencing the feelings I have at this moment: enthusiasm, amazement and intrigue.

We are currently witnessing history unfold. Disclosure is taking place at this moment. It's not complete by any means. We don't possess all the answers, but it is occurring.

You are involved in this. You know about it. It's on your mind. You're seeking answers.

That makes a big difference. You are here.

What steps should we take next? How can we move forward with this understanding?

This is what we'll discuss in the following chapter. Our concluding discussion. Where we bring everything together.

Come on, buddy. Let's have that conversation.

CHAPTER 8

SO... WHAT NOW?

Hi there, my Amazing Beautiful Wonderful friend! Great to meet you again!

We've shared quite an adventure together haven't we?

Lets reflect on our starting point. All the way back in Chapter 1, we discussed ancient civilizations, we talked about the Sumerians and Egyptians, the Nazca Lines, remarkable accuracy in construction projects and sudden progress.

Next we explored scriptures such as the Bible, the Quran, Hindu texts, and Buddhist cosmology, discovering accounts of sky beings that closely resemble what we would identify as aliens nowadays.

We followed reports across the ages: Nuremberg in 1561, the Great Airship Wave of the 1890s, the Battle of Los Angeles in 1942, and the Ghost Rockets over Scandinavia in 1946.

We saw the trend of denial surface with Roswell in 1947. Project Sign's rejected conclusion that UFOs originated from outer space.

We analyzed military incidents, including Rendlesham Forest. We had the Phoenix Lights, the USS Nimitz "Tic Tac" event, and the USS Roosevelt incident, all supported by numerous eyewitnesses, sensor readings and official paperwork.

Lastly, we reached the topic of disclosure: hearings in Congress, Pentagon documents, credible whistleblowers providing testimony under oath. It's been really intense!

What a fabulous journey it has been! Now we're nearing the conclusion of the book sharing our last conversation.

So pour yourself a cup of coffee or tea or bourbon. Take a seat. Let's talk like two pals who have just witnessed an astonishing story.

Except it's not fiction. It's real. It's all real.

What You Won't See (A Reality Check)

Okay, now I gotta be totally upfront and real with you.

Just because you read this book (thank you, BTW) it doesn't

mean you're suddenly going to see UFOs everywhere.

You most likely will not find a spaceship floating around your backyard. You won't experience a close encounter during your commute to work tomorrow. You won't awaken to find extraterrestrials standing at the end of your bed... actually, that would be pretty horrifying!

This isn't Harry Potter. You haven't suddenly found out that you're a wizard and that you're surrounded by magic.

In reality, the vast majority of people will never witness a UFO. Most will spend their lives without having a personal encounter... and that is perfectly fine! That's totally normal.

This book wasn't intended to transform you into a UFO hunter or to make you paranoid or perpetually watching the skies for strange lights.

So WTH was this book about?

It was all about seeing the patterns and *opening your mind.*

It was about showing you what's been happening throughout human history and what's still happening today.

The point was to let you know there's a larger narrative unfolding, a narrative that has been intentionally concealed, ignored and mocked for years.

The goal was to assist you in realizing that a significant question confronts humanity... "Are we alone?" And that answer appears to be "No way, José."

This book focused on knowledge and awareness. It encourages you to think past and to challenge the accepted stories you've been told throughout your life.

Most importantly, it aimed at assisting you in realizing that this is the discussion we ought to be engaging in. Not some trivial celebrity scandal or the hottest new Netflix binge. Not some fabricated outrage trending on social media platforms.

This! We should all be talking about <u>this</u>!

Why <u>This</u> Matters So Much

Can I be real blunt with you for a second?

The biggest event in human history has been unfolding and most people are completely oblivious to it.

They focus more on celebrity rumors than on the Pentagon's acknowledgment that UFOs are visiting us.

They are more engaged with the latest reality TV saga than with Congressional sessions where military employees swear they had encounters with technology that is not supposed to be real.

They focus on which Netflix or HBO shows to watch next rather than considering the chance that we might not be the only intelligent beings in the universe.

And I understand... Truly, I do. The everyday routine can be extremely draining. It's so much easier to immerse yourself in entertainment than to confront unsettling issues. Celebrity gossip and streaming series offer comfort and familiarity. They don't challenge your world view.

But come on. Aren't you getting tired of it? Don't you yearn for something more?

Aren't you tired of the distraction machine? Of being fed trivial nonsense while real, profound, world-changing things are happening?

<u>This</u> matters. <u>This</u> is what we should be talking about.

What's at stake here is the confirmation that we are not alone as intelligent beings in the universe. That there exist others who have been coming to us, watching us, possibly even attempting to communicate with us, or guide us in some manner.

This is quite possibly the most important realization humanity has ever faced or ever will face.

What's Out There

Lets discuss the significance of this and consider the consequences.

If these UFOs are real, and all the data indicates they are, then what is their origin? Who constructed them?

Are they extraterrestrial? From another planet in our galaxy or beyond? Could they be from another dimension? Perhaps a parallel one? Another realm beyond our comprehension?

Could they be travelers through time? People from the future returning to witness events in our past? Perhaps future humans have evolved and no longer resemble current humans, leading us to mistake them for extraterrestrials from a distant planet?

We don't know for certain. However, based upon the behavior of these flying objects, it is highly possible that they are extraterrestrial.

Which means: **Other advanced civilizations exist.**

And if they can build craft that defy our understanding of physics, that can travel between stars, that can operate in our atmosphere and underwater and in space seamlessly... then they're advanced. Like, REALLY advanced.

How advanced exactly? We don't know, but consider this:

Human beings progressed from the first flight in 1903 to reaching the moon in 1969. That span is 66 years. Under a regular human lifespan.

Picture a civilization that has existed for thousands of years, or several billion years. Imagine what their society has achieved during all this time.

The age of our universe is nearly 13.8 billion years. Our Earth is 4.5 billion years old. Modern humans have existed for approx 300,000 years. Civilization, in its current form? About 10,000 years old. Industrial technology? Close to only 250 years.

We are infants. Babies in the cosmos. We've just started to walk. We're still at the drooling phase. Goo-Goo-Ga-Ga!

If there's a civilization out there that's even just 10,000 years older than us, they'd be so far beyond our technology that it would look like magic. Arthur C. Clarke said it best: "Any sufficiently advanced technology is indistinguishable from magic."

Now imagine a civilization a million years ahead. Or ten million. Or a billion.

What could they do? What have they mastered?

Space Travel, Time Travel, and Beyond

If they've figured out how to travel between stars, and they must have, because they're here, then they've mastered energy and propulsion systems we can barely imagine.

If they have discovered a way to journey between stars, and they most certainly have because they are here, then they have perfected energy and propulsion systems which we can barely imagine.

But what else?

Time travel? If you can control spacetime sufficiently to achieve faster-than-light travel, then time manipulation wouldn't be too far-fetched. Einsteins general relativity closely connects space and time. Perhaps they've discovered a method to traverse both?

Inter-dimensional travel? Suppose there are alternate dimensions or parallel universes and those beings have discovered a way to navigate between them? According to string theory, there could be 11 dimensions. We humans only perceive three spatial dimensions plus one dimension of time. What if other beings can access them?

Consciousness and communication? What if they've mastered understanding consciousness itself? What if they can communicate telepathically or interface directly with minds? Many abduction accounts describe communication without words, thoughts being transmitted directly. Is that real? Or is it humans trying to describe something they don't have the framework to understand?

Biological mastery? Assuming the claims regarding "non-human biologics" are true, what implications arise? Are these entities biological, in nature or are they robotic? Could they be cybernetic? Are they AI in physical bodies? Have they completely surpassed biological limitations?

Anything is possible. And that's how it should be considered.

We cannot limit our thinking to what we currently understand. If there is a civilization thats millions of years more advanced than us, their abilities would seem impossible to us right now.

Just as someone living in the year 1500 could not have

conceived the idea of smartphones, airplanes, or the internet, we are unable to envision what an advanced civilization might have accomplished.

That's the truth we must confront. Thats what disclosure means.

What Disclosure Means for Humanity

Here's the hopeful scenario:

The discovery of life might bring humanity together like never before. Instantly all our differences like ethnicity, faith, country, political views, seem insignificant next to the reality that we share this planet. We are all beings. We face this existence collectively. President Ronald Reagan expressed something similar.

It resembles the "overview effect" mentioned by astronauts which is viewing Earth from space makes you understand there are no boundaries or separations. It is just a single stunning planet we all inhabit. Disclosure might bring about that sensation worldwide.

Maybe it forces us to cooperate. Maybe it makes us realize that our survival and flourishing depend on working together rather than fighting each other.

Maybe it inspires us. Maybe knowing that advanced civilizations exist gives us hope that we can evolve beyond our current problems. That we can survive our adolescence as a species and grow into something greater.

That's the best-case scenario. And it's possible.

Maybe it compels us to cooperate with each other. Perhaps it helps us understand that our existence and prosperity rely on unity rather than on conflict.

Maybe it motivates and inspires us. Perhaps the awareness that advanced civilizations are there offers us hope that we can overcome our present challenges. That we can get through our species and develop into something extraordinary.

That's the best-case scenario. And it's possible.

What You Can Do

So here's where it gets intimate and personal. What do you do with this information? How do you move forward?

Stay Open-Minded (But Not So Open Your Brain Falls Out)

There's a balance here. You want to be open to possibilities, to new ideas, to paradigm-shifting realities. The universe is stranger than we imagined, and we need to be willing to accept that.

But you also need to maintain critical thinking. Not every UFO story is real. Not every witness is credible. Not every photo is authentic. There's a lot of noise out there—hoaxes, mis-identifications, attention-seekers, scammers.

A great balance exists in this situation. It's important to remain receptive to possibilities, new concepts and paradigm-shifting realities. The universe is more peculiar than we thought. We must be prepared to embrace that.

However it is essential to maintain critical thinking. Not all UFO accounts are genuine. Not every eyewitness is trustworthy. Not every image is genuine. There is a big deal of interference like frauds, mistaken identities, hoaxes, attention grabbers, and con-artists.

So be open-minded, but critical. Extraordinary claims require extraordinary evidence. Don't believe something just because it fits the story you want to believe. Insist on proof and evidence.

The objective is to discover truth not to validate notions.

Educate Yourself

If you want to go deeper into this topic, there are resources available:

Declassified documents: The Black Vault (theblackvault.com) hosts a collection of declassified government documents on UFOs. You can read them yourself.

Scientific organizations: The Scientific Coalition for UAP Studies (SCU) uses scientific methodology approaches to examine UFO data. Their analyses are detailed and trustworthy.

Credible researchers: Look for people with credentials, with access to primary sources, who apply strict methods. Stay away from conspiracy theorists who make wild claims without evidence.

Congressional hearings: Watch them yourself. Avoid depending on reports. Listen to the testimony of witnesses.

Books and documentaries: There are good ones and bad ones. Be discerning. Choose those that reference sources, recognize uncertainties, and avoid making assertions that exceed the supporting evidence.

Educate yourself. Become informed. Be part of the conversation in a meaningful way.

Keep Looking Up

And finally: look up at the sky a little differently now. Not obsessively, but with a sense of wonder.

The sky is not simply vacant air overhead. It serves as a backdrop where this mystery unfolds. It is the boundary where mankind encounters the unfamiliar.

Chances are you won't encounter a UFO, but you are aware that it can happen. You are aware that others have witnessed them. You are aware that something exists beyond.

That shifts your perspective on the world.

A Personal Note

Look, I want to express my gratitude for accompanying me on this path. For reading this book. For being willing to engage with ideas that challenge everything we've been taught.

This isn't just some interesting topic for me. This is something that matters deeply. It could change everything about how humanity sees itself and its position in the cosmos.

I understand it's overwhelming and a great deal to take in. However, I truly hope that I have expanded your perspective, even just a little bit.

We are currently experiencing something. We are observing a time when humanity embarks on its significant advance, recognizing that we are not isolated and that the universe is immense and enigmatic and that we belong to something far greater than just ourselves.

That's amazing. That's beautiful. That's definitely cause for celebration. Cheers, friend!

See You Out There

Alright, my friend. This is the point where we go our own paths. At least for the time being.

I hope this journey is just beginning for you. I wish you continue to explore and continue to to gaze at the heavens.

Who can say? Maybe one day when everything is fully revealed and the truth emerges, we'll reflect back on this time. Understand: we witnessed it. We played a role. We were the ones who refused to turn away and accept the lies, who persistently sought the answers.

That's something to be proud of.

So thank you. Thank you for reading. Thank you for thinking. Thank you for being willing to engage with the biggest mystery humanity has ever faced.

The visitors from above are real.

They've been here all along.

At last we are prepared to recognize it.

Keep looking up, my Beautiful, Wonderful friend.

The sky is full of possibilities.

See you out there, sky observer!

The journey continues.

But for now...it's **The End.**

ABOUT THE AUTHOR:

American-Pakistani author Adil Bhatti has long felt drawn to the unexplained world of UFOs and the probability of life beyond Earth. Convinced that we are not alone, he writes with curiosity and conviction about the hidden truths that may soon come to light. He believes disclosure is closer than anyone realizes, and the signs have been with us all along. For inquiries, please reach out at alpstudiollc@gmail.com or Instagram/Threads @6MillionRupeeMan

www.ingramcontent.com/pod-product-compliance
Lightning Source LLC
Chambersburg PA
CBHW070628030426
42337CB00020B/3949